Curriculum Focus

The Victorians

Elizabeth Hoad

HOPSCOTCH

A division of MA Education Ltd

HOPSCOTCH

Published by Hopscotch,
a division of MA Education,
St Jude's Church, Dulwich Road,
London, SE24 0PB
www.hopscotchbooks.com
020 7738 5454

© 2010 MA Education Ltd.

Written by Elizabeth Hoad
Designed and illustrated by Emma Turner
Front cover illustration by Yana Elkassova

ISBN 978 1 90539 080 9

Contents

Cross-curricular links

Chapter	History SoW	Geography SoW	PSHE and citizenship	Literacy framework	DT (Sow)	ICT SoW
1	Unit 11			Y5 Non-fiction, Unit 2 Y6 Non-fiction, Unit 1		Unit 2C Unit 4A
2	Unit 11		Unit 7	Y5 Narrative, Unit 4 Y5 Non-fiction, Unit 3 Y6 Non-fiction, Unit 1 Y6 Non-fiction, Unit 3		Unit 6D
3	Unit 11			Y5 Non-fiction, Unit 2	5c	Unit 4A Unit 6D
4	Unit 11		Unit 8	Y5 Non-fiction, Unit 2		Unit 6A
5	Unit 12	Unit 6 Unit 18 Unit 24	Unit 5 Unit 9	Y6 Non-fiction, Unit 3		Unit 6A
6	Unit 12	Unit 24	Unit 5 Unit 9	Y5 Non-fiction, Unit 1		Unit 6D
7	Unit 11			Y6 Narrative, Unit 4 Y6 Non-fiction, Unit 2		Unit 6D
8	Unit 11			Y5 Non-fiction, Units 1 and 2	5c	Unit 4A
9	Unit 11			Y5 Non-fiction, Units 2 and 3 Y6 Non-fiction, Unit 2		Unit 6D
10	Unit 12	Unit 6 Unit 18 Unit 24	Unit 5 Unit 9	Y5 Non-fiction, Unit 2	4a 5a	Unit 5A

Introduction

Each chapter in this book has an initial set of background teacher's notes to give you the basic information you need to teach each aspect of the subject. After this there are Generic sheets which can be copied or displayed to illustrate different aspects of Victorian life. Then there is a lesson plan which gives you guidance on how to teach each aspect and how to support and extend the children's learning. Finally there are photocopiable and differentiated activity sheets for the children to complete in groups or individually.

Each chapter in this book looks at different aspects of the lives of the Victorians. They are based on the QCA Schemes of Work for History at Key Stage 2, years 5 and 6. They cover the minutiae of the life of Victorian children from their living conditions, education and leisure time to the global achievements of the Industrial Revolution and the legacy they have left behind. The impact of these wider changes on ordinary people is investigated as well. The children are encouraged to find out about the way in which our lives continue to be shaped and influenced by the Victorians. The final chapter in the book is based on the children looking at their local environment to find any evidence that remains of the Victorians.

The chapters do not need to be followed in any particular order and the activities should be considered as starting points for further investigation. You will need to adapt some of the activities according to the area you live in. If you are fortunate enough to live close to any working museums spend as much time as possible actively investigating the world of the nineteenth century.

The Victorian age was a time of great change and innovation which impacted on the lives of everyone. The class divide was clear and social hierarchy was observed strictly. A strict moral code was followed by the majority of the population as the Church had a very strong influence on the behaviour of rich and poor alike. Those who were seen to have strayed from the straight and narrow were condemned and forgiveness was not easily obtained.

The reign of Queen Victoria was the longest of any monarch to date and she was a much beloved figure. Despite her withdrawal from public life after Prince Albert's death she was still a figure of respect and she was the figurehead of the British Empire. It is perhaps at this time that Britain enjoyed its greatest influence and wealth. Our status amongst other world powers in modern times is perhaps still influenced by our past.

There were many highly respected and revered figures who were alive during Victoria's reign and whose work and successes have affected many things we take for granted in our modern world. Men and women such as Dr. Barnardo, Florence Nightingale and Isambard Kingdom Brunel have to a lesser or greater degree shaped the modern world and in some cases the results of their work is in evidence on a daily basis.

CHAPTER 1

Victoria and her children

Victoria the Princess

Queen Victoria was the niece of William IV and reigned from 1837 to 1901. She is the longest reigning monarch of the United Kingdom to date and during her reign it was a time of tremendous change.

Princess Alexandrina Victoria was born on May 24th 1819 in Kensington Palace. Her mother was a German princess and her father was Edward, Duke of Kent, the fourth son of King George III. His brother was Prince Regent and was crowned George IV in 1820. Victoria's father died in debt soon after she was born and her mother nearly had to return to Germany. Her brother Prince Leopold of Saxe-Coburg gave her an allowance so they were able to stay. In 1825 Parliament acknowledged that Victoria would be likely to accede to the throne, because William IV had no legitimate children living, and gave an annuity of £6000 to pay for her education and keep.

As a child Victoria had quite a fiery temper until her governess Baroness Lehzen was able to "tame" her and she grew up to be a polite young woman. Her uncle Prince Leopold took a great interest in her as she grew up until he became King of Belgium in 1831. Her mother shielded her from many of her other relatives, both English and German, because she considered their behaviour to be inappropriate. Her mother controlled her every move until she became Queen, when she finally asserted her authority and independence. Up until that time Victoria had always slept in a little bed in her mother's room and when she became Queen and moved to Buckingham Palace she immediately ordered that they had separate apartments and her mother had to send a note to ask permission to see her daughter.

Victoria the Queen

Victoria became Queen when she was eighteen. Royalty came of age three years before other people at that time. She made an instant impression on all around her from the first day and showed her strong will and obstinacy. She carried out her royal duties with the Prime Minister with unexpected efficiency and maturity. She asked Baroness Lehzen to stay in court and help her, and she had two trusted advisers in her early reign, Baron Stockmar and the Prime Minister Lord Melbourne. Lord Palmerston, who was Foreign Secretary, was also very important in guiding her in the early days.

Throughout her reign she was devoted to her country although she was sheltered from much of the unpleasantness of life in the nineteenth century. She was unaware of the living conditions of the majority of the population but despite this she was well loved by her subjects.

Victoria and Albert

Victoria's uncle Leopold set up a meeting between Victoria and her cousin Albert, Prince of Saxe-Coburg-Gotha in May 1836. They married on 10th February 1840 and were devoted to one another. Albert was very handsome but was also intelligent and had strong principles. He was a good foil to the more frivolous Victoria and they settled into a happy family life. Victoria gradually allowed Albert to take on more and more of her responsibilities as Queen and in 1857 he was given the title 'Prince Consort'.

Albert died in 1861 after contracting typhoid fever. He was aged 42 and Victoria and Albert had enjoyed 21 years of marriage. Victoria went into a period of deep mourning and neglected her duties for many years. She withdrew to Balmoral for a long time and the monarch's powers declined and were taken on by the Prime Minister and ruling party of the time. She wore black for the rest of her life and when she returned to her public duties she refused to wear her robes of state or her crown.

Victoria's children

Victoria had nine children, forty grandchildren and thirty-seven great grandchildren. She was known as the "Grandmother of Europe" because so many of them married members of other European royal families.

Her eldest child, the Princess Royal, was called Victoria and was born in 1840. She married Frederick III, German Emperor and King of Prussia.

Albert Edward, Prince of Wales, was born in 1841 and married Princess Alexandra of Denmark. He became King (Edward VII) in 1901 when he was sixty. He was known for bringing a spirit of harmony between France and England during his reign. He was a very popular king despite never being involved with any affairs of State while his mother was alive.

Victoria's third child, Alice, was born in 1842 and she married the Grand Duke Ludwig of Hesse. Alfred was born in 1844 and he married the Grand Duchess Marie of Russia. Helena, born in 1846, married Prince Christian of Schleswig Holstein. Louise who was born in 1848 married the Marquis of Lorne; Arthur, born in 1850, married Princess Louise of Prussia; and Leopold, 1853, married Princess Helena of Waldeck. Finally her youngest child Beatrice, born in 1857, married Prince Henry of Battenberg.

Both Victoria and Albert spent a lot of time with their children and were determined to bring them up as normally as possible. They spent their holidays at Balmoral or at Osborne House on the Isle of Wight. Not all of the children were as serious-minded as their father. Their eldest son, Bertie, was a bit of a playboy and caused them much concern and disquiet in his youth. The Queen condemned Bertie's behaviour, and she blamed him for Albert's death. She believed that the shock of hearing of his affair with an actress caused Albert's final illness.

The end of Victoria's Reign

After Albert's death Victoria withdrew from the public eye and grieved for many years on her own at Balmoral or Osborne House. Her popularity waned during this time as did her power over the government. It wasn't until Bertie became ill with typhoid fever in 1871 that public sympathy turned in her favour again. When he recovered the nation was most definitely behind their Queen once more.

In 1876 Benjamin Disraeli, who was then Prime Minister, passed a Bill in Parliament, which meant that Victoria became Empress of India. England became the centre of a huge Empire during her reign and when she died she ruled over one quarter of the world.

Her Golden Jubilee was celebrated in 1887 and her Diamond Jubilee in 1897 with much pomp and circumstance. The entire country joined in the celebrations at that time, and when she died in 1901 they went into mourning. Children wore black and Englishmen all over the world bought black edged handkerchiefs. She was finally laid to rest in the mausoleum at Frogmore, Windsor, beside Prince Albert.

Important dates

1819	Princess Alexandrina Victoria born
1821	First female doctor born, Dr. Elizabeth Blackwell
1825	Stephenson drove first steam locomotive from Stockton to Darlington
1829	Stephenson's "Rocket" Foundation of the Metropolitan police force
1830	First steam fire engine
1832	Lewis Carroll born
1833	Abolition of slavery in British colonies
1835	Town councils allowed to set up their own police forces
1837	Victoria becomes Queen Shorthand invented by Isaac Pitman Morse code alphabet adopted
1840	Queen Victoria married Prince Albert Penny post began Thomas Hardy born
1841	Thomas Cook's travel agency founded
1845	Irish potato famine
1846	Planet Neptune discovered
1847	Chloroform first used as an anaesthetic in Britain 10-Hour Act introduced
1850	William Wordsworth died Robert Louis Stevenson born
1851	The Great Exhibition J.M.W. Turner died
1854-6	Crimean War
1855	Charlotte Brontë died
1856	Victoria Cross first given George Bernard Shaw born
1858	First message sent by Atlantic cable
1859	Darwin's "Origin of Species" published
1860	Training of nurses in Britain began
1861	Prince Albert died Abolition of slavery in USA
1864	International Red Cross started
1865	Lister introduced antiseptic surgery
1866	H.G. Wells born
1869	Suez Canal opened Sir Henry Wood born
1870	Education Act Charles Dickens died
1871	Trade Unions legalised First FA Cup competition
1873	Sir Edwin Landseer died
1874	First typewriter for sale
1876	Telephone invented by Alexander Graham Bell
1878	First electric lighting Microphone invented by David Hughes
1879	Albert Einstein born
1881	Fleming born
1883	First match between Australia and England for the Ashes
1887	Golden Jubilee celebrations
1888	Edward Lear died
1890	Forth Bridge opened
1891	Education became free
1892	Alfred, Lord Tennyson died
1894	Opening of Manchester Ship Canal
1895	X-rays discovered
1897	Diamond Jubilee celebrations
1899	Boer War started First international wireless message sent by Marconi
1901	Death of Queen Victoria

LESSON PLAN

Victoria and her children

Unit 11 What was it like for children living in Victorian times?
Who were the Victorians and when did they live?
• to identify Queen Victoria and place the Victorian period in relation to other periods of British history
• to infer information from a portrait

Resources

• String, pegs, illustrated dated cards to represent different periods of history.

• Copies of portraits of Queen Victoria, her family, and paintings of events that they attended, such as the Great Exhibition.

• Generic sheet 1

• Interactive whiteboard or OHP

• Activity sheets 1–3

Starting points: whole class

Ask the children what they already know about Queen Victoria and the Victorians and record all the things they tell you. This information will be worth revisiting at the end of the topic to see if they have learned more detail or if what they knew was accurate. It is worth understanding and exploring their pre-conceptions about a period of history as well as establishing where there is already underlying knowledge that you can build upon.

The aim of this unit of work is to place the Victorian era within a timeframe to help the children understand when it was. They need to understand that while the longest reigning monarch to date was on the throne life in Britain changed dramatically. The children also need to observe and think about how the queen herself changed over time and how the world was at the beginning and end of her life.

The Victorian era lasted from 1837 to 1901 when Queen Victoria died aged 81. Ask the children to work out how long she was on the throne and put this into context by thinking about the ages of their parents and grandparents. Suspend a "washing line" from the ceiling of the classroom, and attach a card with the current date at one end of the string with a peg. Add cards to mark the change of each century ensuring that they are evenly spaced along the timeline. Remind the children of other historical times they have investigated during Key Stage 1 and 2 already. Using these dates give the children illustrated and dated cards to place on the string in the correct position along the

timeline. They will need to think about the year(s) marked on each of the cards and work out how far apart they will need to be on the string. You might choose to label the change from B.C. to A.D. as well to extend the children. Once all these periods of time are positioned appropriately on the timeline ask the children questions about how long it was between specific eras, for example, are we closer in history to the Victorians than the Tudors to the Victorians, and so on. Leave this visual timeline up for the duration of the topic so the children can remind themselves of when the Victorians featured in the history of Britain. You could add more specific detail relevant to the Victorians as time goes on if you like.

Display Generic sheet 1 to show the Kings and Queens of England and when they reigned. Ask them to locate Queen Victoria, Queen Elizabeth II and any other monarchs they are familiar with from other history topics.

Find some large colour copies of portraits of Queen Victoria and ask the children if they know who it is. Do they think they are of the same person? Once they have had a chance to look at these and discussed them for a little while start them off on their activity sheets.

Group activities

Activity sheet 1
This sheet is for children who need a little more support. They need to look at the two pictures of Queen Victoria, and then comment on her appearance and how it has changed over time.

Activity sheet 2
This sheet is for children who are more confident and work independently. They need to look at the two pictures of Queen Victoria and choose words to describe her appearance before writing sentences to comment on her appearance and how it has changed over time.

Activity sheet 3
This sheet is for the most able children. They will look at the two pictures of Queen Victoria and comment on them and then use non-fiction texts to find more information about her life at that time.

Plenary session

Ask the children which of the two portraits they prefer and why. Ask them to put copies of the portraits on the timeline above them so they can see how the Queen herself changed over time. Ask them if they have a better understanding of the length of time the Victorian era covered.

Ideas for support

If the children are struggling with the concept of a timeline draw a simple line with the important time periods demarcated on it. Talk them through the periods of history they have already studied and ensure they understand the relative timescale between the current year and Tudor times, the Victorians and so on.

When they are looking at the portraits of Victoria it may help to tell the children when they were painted and how old the Queen was at that time. Give them a bit of basic information about her life at that time to help them appreciate why she is looking stern and so on.

Ideas for extension

Give the children a simple blank family tree that takes them back to their great great grandparents' generation and ask them to see how much of this they can fill in at home. See if they can manage to get back to the Victorians in

their own family. If they can do this and know what their jobs were the children could research that particular job and find out about what they did and what their living conditions were like.

The children can also see if they can find other portraits of Victoria and her family at different stages of their lives. The National Portrait Gallery website has some excellent photos which would be useful for the children to look at, as does their website. The children could date each of the portraits they see and work out when it was painted during her reign.

Linked ICT activities

The children should use an online encyclopaedia, such as Wikipedia, or similar software, to research the lives of Queen Victoria and her family. They should search for one specific family member and use a word processing package such as Microsoft Word to record the information they find. Teach the children to cut and paste pictures and information in order to produce a piece of information text that could be displayed in the classroom or made into a reference book that the whole class can access easily.

There is software available for making family trees such as "Legacy". The children may already be aware of some of this software if their family are involved in investigating their family history. Invite someone in to demonstrate how such software works, or ask the children to use it at home if possible, to develop their own family trees.

Kings and Queens of England

Roman Britain	43-450 A.D.	Henry VIII	1509
Division into Kingdoms	613-1017	Edward VI	1547
Danish Rule	1017-1066	Mary I	1553
William I	1066	Elizabeth I	1558
William II	1087	James I	1603
Henry I	1100	Charles I	1625
Stephen	1135	Commonwealth	1649
Henry II	1154	Charles II	1660
Richard I	1189	James II	1685
John	1199	William III and Mary II	1689
Henry III	1216	Anne	1702
Edward I	1272	George I	1714
Edward II	1307	George II	1727
Edward III	1327	George III	1760
Richard II	1377	George IV	1820
Henry IV	1399	William IV	1830
Henry V	1413	Victoria	1837
Henry VI	1422	Edward VII	1901
Edward IV	1461	George V	1910
Edward V	1483	Edward VIII	1936
Richard III	1483	George VI	1936
Henry VII	1485	Elizabeth II	1952

Queen Victoria

Name ....

1. Which of these words best describes the Queen in the first picture?
   Circle the ones which are most suitable.

young	old	regal	fun-loving	pretty	attractive
confident	serious	sad	angry	full of life	unhappy
slim	large	ordinary	important	sensible	happy

2. Which of these words best describes the Queen in the second picture?
   Circle the ones which are most suitable.

young	old	regal	fun-loving	pretty	attractive
confident	serious	sad	angry	full of life	unhappy
slim	large	ordinary	important	sensible	happy

3. Now cut out the first picture and stick it onto a piece of paper. Using the words you have circled write some sentences about the young Queen.

4. Do the same with the second picture.

5. Would you most like to meet the young or old Queen and why?
   Write a sentence to explain this.

   _____

   _____

   _____

Queen Victoria

Name

1. Write some words that best describe the young Queen in the first picture.

_____

_____

_____

2. Write some words that best describe the Queen in the second picture.

_____

_____

_____

3. Now cut out the first picture and stick it onto a piece of paper. Using the words you have recorded write some sentences about the young Queen.

4. Do the same with the second picture.

5. Would you most like to meet the young or old Queen and why? Write a sentence to explain this. _____

_____

Queen Victoria

Name ....

1. Cut out each picture of the Queen and describe the appearance of Queen Victoria in each of the pictures using full sentences.

2. Use information texts to find out roughly how old she was in each portrait and what her life was like at that time.

3. Compare the two portraits and say which one is most interesting to you and why.

4. Look at the portraits and decide which of the two you would trust the most to run and represent our country. Give reasons why.

5. Can you find another portrait from the middle period of her life? Compare this with the other two and write about how the Queen's life changed.

Social reformers

Famous Victorians

The Victorian era produced men and women who changed lives and attitudes dramatically and irrevocably. Many of these people are household names and their legacy continues today, for example, through the charity Barnardos. It is important for the children to learn about some of these people and their impact on the lives of the rich and poor. This chapter focuses on three principal characters, Lord Shaftesbury, Dr. Barnardo and Charles Dickens. In order to understand some of the living and working conditions at the time it is vital to learn something of the work carried out by these men.

Other characters, whose impact on Victorian life was very important, such as Isambard Kingdom Brunel and Florence Nightingale, will be mentioned in later chapters.

Lord Shaftesbury (1801-1885)

In the 1800s many of the factory workers were children. They were poorly paid and treated badly but they had to work in order to help their families to survive. Children as young as five were sent to work for more than ten hours a day and many people considered this to be normal and acceptable. Children in the country generally had a much easier life than those in towns as they lived in better surroundings on the whole and didn't work until they were much older.

However, many families migrated to towns and cities to work as the pay was better than farm labouring. Children in factories were working in noisy, dangerous conditions and there were accidents and fatalities quite often. The overseers who watched their work were often quite harsh and demanded a lot from adults and children alike. Small boys were employed by Master Sweeps to climb up inside the chimneys and sweep them out by hand, and young children were often sent down into mines. Many families could not afford to keep their children at home or send them to school.

In 1836 birth certificates became compulsory so it was easier to check whether a child was underage or not. The first factory laws that were brought in did not go far enough to protect working children and there were not enough factory inspectors to make sure that the rules were followed. In 1842 a law was passed which prevented women and little girls from working in the mines and boys had to be at least ten before they were allowed to go down into the pits. Lord Shaftesbury became a Tory MP in 1836 and he was instrumental in the establishing and passing of many of these reforms, including reducing working hours to ten hours for children.

Lord Shaftesbury was chairman of the Ragged Schools Union which set up schools in the 1840s to provide a free education to children in many of the poorest areas of industrial towns. These schools also provided food, clothing and shelter for many children.

Shaftesbury worked tirelessly to get legislation through to protect children until eventually in 1880 the Government made it compulsory for all children aged between 5 and 10 to go to school. He became known as 'The Children's Friend' for the work he did to improve working conditions for children.

Dr. Barnardo

Thomas John Barnardo (1845-1905) was encouraged in his work by Lord Shaftesbury's influence. He trained as a doctor and intended to work as a foreign medical missionary. He worked in the East End of London during the cholera epidemic of 1866 and it was during this time that he realised the full scale of deprivation and homelessness amongst children in that area. He opened his first home in 1870 in London and at the time of his death there were 112 homes for children. Their main aim was to provide food, clothes and an education for homeless children. Barnardo also insisted on giving the children a religious education as well, with the children following the protestant faith. In 1876 he and his wife opened up "The Girls Village Home" in Essex which he hoped would replicate village life for them. This expanded over the years and ultimately housed 1,300 girls in 1906.

Barnardo's work continues to this day through the charity named after him. The charity continues its work not only with children without families but also with victims of abuse. The charity has a resource pack available about Victorian Britain which contains copies of original photos and archive material from Barnardo himself.

Charles Dickens

Charles Dickens the well-known novelist (1812-1870) was also involved in social reform and was often an outspoken critic of living and working conditions in Victorian Britain. The characters in his novels were usually ordinary working-class people and he wrote about how they lived. He commented on many aspects of Victorian life that he felt people should be fully aware of, for example, prisons, bad schools, the workhouse and the general plight of the poor. In many respects he was like a modern investigative journalist as he brought people's attention to the things he felt needed to be changed. He hoped public opinion would be changed or awakened by what he wrote. Many of the things he wrote about are still relevant and valid even in modern society and this is possibly one of the reasons why his works have never been out of print.

Dickens' novel "David Copperfield" is largely autobiographical and mirrors much of what happened to Dickens during his early life. His father was sent to the debtor's prison, the Marshalsea (which features in "Little Dorrit") when Charles was twelve. Shortly before this happened Charles was sent to work in a blacking factory for ten-hour days pasting labels on jars of shoe polish. This work paid for his rent and helped support the rest of his family who were in the Marshalsea. However, when his father was released his mother made him continue to work at the factory as well as attending school. His bad experiences there were reflected in his portrayal of the school which David Copperfield attends. As a young man he went on to work in a law office as a junior clerk until he eventually became a freelance journalist. Dickens' first love,

Maria Beadnell, was sent away to Paris when their attachment became known and it is believed that Dora in "David Copperfield" is based on her.

Dickens married his wife Catherine in 1836 and they had ten children. They separated in 1858 when he formed a close bond with an actress, Ellen Ternan. Divorce was not an option in Victorian times and he continued to support his wife and children financially for the rest of his life.

Dickens' novels were serialised and published monthly with a cliffhanger at the end of each instalment. Unlike many other authors he wrote each book in chronological order as they were published. His work was so popular, and, in the absence of other forms of entertainment they became the soap operas of his age. In his later life he embarked on a series of readings in theatres all over the country and in the United States of America.

Social reformers

Unit 11 What was it like for children living in Victorian times?
Who were the Victorians and when did they live?
Who helped to improve the lives of Victorian children?
How did life change for children living in Victorian Britain?
• to consider what life was like for children in the past
• to understand that the work of individuals can change aspects of society
• to find out about important figures in Victorian times
• to recall information about the life of children in Victorian times
• to select appropriate material and present it in a way that shows their understanding of the Victorian period

Resources

• Illustration of children working or living in the streets – generic sheets 1-4

• Copy of the United Nations Rights of the Child (see the Unicef website www.unicef.org)

• Activity sheets 1-3

• Abridged versions of Charles Dickens' novels

• Scissors and glue

Starting points: Whole Class

Spend some time talking to the children about their lives in the 21st Century and list all the activities they do each day however mundane it may appear to them. Ask them what they think ordinary working class Victorian children did each day. They may possibly never have considered that some children their age could have already been working for several years and would never have learned to read or write. Teach the children about what life was like for many children and the sort of work they had to do from an early age. Show them illustrations on the generic sheets of children working in various different scenarios and discuss what they can see. Work out how long a ten hour day is with reference to the things they do each day. Share their thoughts about how they would feel if they had to work that long every single day with only one day off a week if they were lucky.

Discuss what they consider to be their rights and look at the United Nations Rights for Children. Compare their rights as a child to those of Victorian children.

Spend some time doing some role-play activities as factory workers and overseers and get them to try to imagine some of the conditions they would be surrounded by on a daily basis.

Split the class into two and sit them opposite one another in the classroom. One half of them are factory owners who are trying to make a living and the other half are social reformers. Initiate a debate between the two to try to get the children to understand how each side stood on the issue of child labour and why they used them. Once they have had a chance to argue both sides talk to the children about whether the factory owners were wrong, or whether they just didn't know any better.

Group activities

Activity sheet 1
This sheet is for children who need a little more support. Show them the sheet with the three social reformers illustrated and read them the information on the sheet if they need help with the text. Talk to the children about what they have learned from the facts they have read. Can they précis the information? As a group read through the text one more time and highlight key points and words that they feel are important. Using these highlighted points ask them to write a couple of sentences about each of the characters. Cut out each picture and stick it next to the relevant piece of writing.

Activity sheet 2
This sheet is for children who are more confident and work independently. Give the children the sheet to read through as a group. Ask them to highlight the key words in each section of the text and then write their own paragraph about each of the social reformers. Cut out each picture and stick it next to the relevant piece of writing.

Activity sheet 3
This sheet is for the most able children. Ask the children to read the sheet through on their own. Get them to highlight the key words in each section of the text and then write their own paragraph about each of the social reformers. Cut out each picture and stick it next to the relevant piece of writing. Encourage them to form their own opinion of

these men and write about which of them they think made the most difference to Victorian children's lives.

Plenary session

Ask the children if they can summarise the important work that Dr. Barnardo, Lord Shaftesbury and Charles Dickens carried out and why it made a difference. Ask them whether they think Charles Dickens' role was as important as the others.

Ideas for support

For children who do not understand about how hard some Victorian children's lives were spend more time looking at the generic sheets and ask them to describe what they can see. Encourage them to imagine themselves in that situation and how they would feel about being unable to play or go to school as they do now. Try to get them to think about how a child's life was about survival and that they didn't have the leisure time, or, the opportunity to develop their skills as modern children do.

Ideas for extension

There are a number of extension activities you can provide for the children. Once they have carried out the previous activities ask them to imagine they are a working class Victorian child. They could write a piece about a day in their lives as a factory worker or a chimney sweep. They could follow this up by writing a plea for improving working conditions as if they were one of the social reformers. Once they have done this they could stand in front of the class to address them as if they are in Parliament or as if they are trying to speak to members of the public to get them to understand what life is like for many children.

The children might be interested in finding out more about Dickens' stories. There are numerous abridged versions of his novels available. Read them a child's version of David Copperfield and then ask them to make up a comic strip to retell part of the story.

Linked ICT activities

The BBC website for schools about Victorian Britain has some fun games and information for the children to access and learn about the working lives of children in Victorian Britain. Make sure the children access the internet site using a favourites list. There are extension activities that you could give the children to complete once they have read the information and done the quizzes. There are several sections that are relevant to the work in this unit, children in coal mines, children at work and children in factories. Continue this work by using a search engine to find further information and then print a page which is of relevance to the topic.

Social reformers

Name ....

Read each passage through carefully. Highlight the words which you think are the most important. Cut out each of the pictures, stick them on a fresh sheet of paper and write two sentences about each character. Make sure you use the words you have highlighted in each passage.

Lord Shaftesbury

Lord Shaftesbury became a Member of Parliament in 1836. He worked hard to improve working conditions for children in factories. In the 1800s many children worked in factories. Children often worked for more than ten hours a day, six days a week. Factories were noisy and dangerous and there were accidents quite often. Small boys climbed up inside chimneys to sweep them out by hand, and young children were often sent down into mines. Many families could not afford to keep their children at home or send them to school.

Lord Shaftesbury was involved with the Ragged Schools Union which set up schools in the 1840s for children in many of the poorest areas of industrial towns. These schools also gave the children food, clothing and shelter. Shaftesbury worked hard until the Government made it compulsory for all children aged between 5 and 10 to go to school. He became known as 'The Children's Friend' for the work he did to improve working conditions for children.

Dr. Barnardo

Thomas John Barnardo trained as a doctor and wanted to work as a foreign medical missionary. When he worked in the East End of London during the cholera epidemic of 1866 he realised how many children were homeless and living in poverty. He opened his first home for homeless children in 1870 in London. When he died there were 112 homes for children. The main aim was to provide food, clothes and an education for homeless children. Barnardo also gave the children a religious education as well.

Charles Dickens

Charles Dickens wrote many well known books and also helped to improve living and working conditions. The characters in his novels were usually ordinary people and he wrote about how they lived. He wrote about prisons, bad schools, the workhouse and the lives of the poor. The story "David Copperfield" tells the story of many of the things that happened to Dickens during his early life. His father was sent to the Marshalsea prison when Charles was twelve because he had not got enough money to pay his debts. Just before this happened Charles was sent to work in a blacking factory for ten-hour days pasting labels on jars of shoe polish. When his father was released from prison Charles was made to work at the factory as well as attending a school where the boys were treated badly.

Dickens' novels were published once a month with a cliffhanger at the end of each chapter. His work was so popular that he used to read his stories in theatres all over the country and in the United States of America.

Social reformers

Name ....

Read each passage through carefully. Highlight the words which you think are the most important. Cut out each of the pictures, stick them on a fresh sheet of paper and write a paragraph about each character and what they did to improve the lives of Victorian children. Make sure you use the words you have highlighted in each passage.

Lord Shaftesbury

Lord Shaftesbury became a Member of Parliament in 1836. He worked hard to get laws made that improved working conditions for children in factories. In the 1800s many factory workers were children. Children as young as five were sent to work for more than ten hours a day, six days a week. Children in factories worked in noisy, dangerous conditions and there were accidents quite often. Small boys were employed by chimney sweeps to climb up inside and sweep them out by hand, and young children were often sent down into mines. Many families could not afford to keep their children at home or send them to school.

In 1842 a law was passed which stopped women and little girls from working in the mines and boys had to be at least ten before they were allowed to go down into the pits. Lord Shaftesbury worked with the Ragged Schools Union which set up schools in the 1840s for children in many of the poorest areas of industrial towns. These schools also provided food, clothing and shelter for many children.

Shaftesbury worked hard until, in 1880, the Government made it compulsory for all children aged between 5 and 10 to go to school. He became known as 'The Children's Friend' for the work he did to improve working conditions for children.

Dr. Barnardo

Thomas John Barnardo trained as a doctor and wanted to work as a foreign medical missionary. He worked in the East End of London during the cholera epidemic of 1866 and he realised how many children were homeless and living in poverty. He wanted to do something to help so he opened his first home for homeless children in 1870 in London. When he died there were 112 homes for children. The main aim was to provide food, clothes and an education for homeless children. Barnardo also wanted to give the children a religious education as well. The charity Barnardo's continues the work he began in the 1800s.

Charles Dickens

Charles Dickens wrote many well-known stories and was also involved in improving living and working conditions. He wrote about how ordinary people lived. He wrote about prisons, bad schools, the workhouse and the general situation of the poor. His novel "David Copperfield" tells the story of many of the things that happened to Dickens during his early life. His father was sent to the debtor's prison, the Marshalsea, when Charles was twelve. Just before this happened Charles was sent to work in a blacking factory for ten-hour days pasting labels on jars of shoe polish. When his father was released Charles was made to work at the factory as well as attending a school where the boys were treated badly.

Dickens' novels were published once a month with a cliffhanger at the end of each chapter. His work was so popular that he used to read his stories in theatres all over the country and in the United States of America.

Social reformers

Name ....

Read each passage through carefully. Highlight the words which you think are the most important. Cut out each of the pictures, stick them on a fresh sheet of paper and write about the work each of these social reformers carried out. Make sure you use the words you have highlighted. Finally, write about which of these men you think made the most significant difference to children's lives and why.

Lord Shaftesbury

Lord Shaftesbury became a Member of Parliament in 1836. He was very involved in improving working conditions for children in factories. In the 1800s many of the factory workers were children. Children as young as five were sent to work for more than ten hours a day, six days a week. Children in factories were working in noisy, dangerous conditions and there were accidents quite often. Small boys were employed by chimney sweeps to climb up inside and sweep them out by hand, and young children were often sent down into mines. Many families could not afford to keep their children at home or send them to school.

In 1842 a law was passed which prevented women and little girls from working in the mines and boys had to be at least ten before they were allowed to go down into the pits. Lord Shaftesbury helped to set up the Ragged Schools Union which provided schools in the 1840s for children in many of the poorest areas of industrial towns. These schools also provided food, clothing and shelter for many children. Shaftesbury worked hard until in 1880 the Government made it compulsory for all children aged between 5 and 10 to go to school. He became known as 'The Children's Friend' for the work he did to improve working conditions for children.

Dr. Barnardo

Thomas John Barnardo trained as a doctor and intended to work as a foreign medical missionary. He worked in the East End of London during the cholera epidemic of 1866 and he realised how many children were homeless and living in poverty. He opened his first home for homeless children in 1870 in London. When he died there were 112 homes for children. The main aim was to provide food, clothes and an education for homeless children. Barnardo also insisted on giving the children a religious education as well. Barnardo's work continues to this day through the charity named after him.

Charles Dickens

Charles Dickens was a well-known novelist and was also involved in social reform. The characters in his novels were usually ordinary working-class people and he wrote about how they lived. He wrote about prisons, bad schools, the workhouse and the general situation of the poor. His novel "David Copperfield" tells the story of many of the things that happened to Dickens during his early life. His father was sent to the debtor's prison, the Marshalsea, when Charles was twelve. Just before this happened Charles was sent to work in a blacking factory for ten-hour days pasting labels on jars of shoe polish. When his father was released Charles was made to work at the factory as well as attending a school where the boys were treated badly.

Dickens' novels were published once a month with a cliffhanger at the end of each chapter. His work was so popular that he used to read his stories in theatres all over the country and in the United States of America.

Clothing

TEACHERS' NOTES

Victorian clothing

There was a definite distinction between the classes during the Victorian era which was most apparent through their clothing. The rich wore clothes of sumptuous materials and brighter colours than the poor. Those in the worst social position merely wore whatever they were able to find and were rarely able to wash anything. Many poor children had no shoes and had to go barefoot through the filthy streets and at work. It was common practice to hand down clothes from one child to another and all girls learned needlework in order to make their own clothes.

Upper and middle class children

Boys and girls were dressed alike during their early years, and it wasn't until they were around four or five that they were dressed differently. Up until that age both boys and girls wore dresses. If you look at any pictures or old photos of small children from that era it is very hard to tell the gender of the child. Babies from wealthier families used to wear dresses covered with embroidery, lace and frills and were always in white. When babies were taken out they would wear little bonnets or caps and would be pushed in a three or four wheeled perambulator.

Queen Victoria became an unwitting leader of children's fashion after dressing the Prince of Wales in a little sailor suit when he was five. Most little boys and girls wore this sort of outfit as a result, with a dark pair of shorts or skirt, a white shirt with a dark neckerchief and sailor's hat. Even today you often see small boys wearing a variation of this outfit for weddings or special occasions. The other item of clothing which Victoria influenced was the wearing of kilts. She loved to wear tartan and consequently kilts became very popular for little girls towards the end of the century.

Boys tended to wear long, dark shorts or trousers with long socks and boots. They then wore a shirt which often had pin tucks or gathering at the neck with a short jacket. Braces or suspenders were used to hold up their trousers and were worn over the shirt. When going outside it was not considered decent to go without a hat and boys used to wear little flat caps or straw hats. Another very popular outfit for boys was known as the Fauntleroy suit. This became popular after the publication of Frances Hodgson Burnett's story "Little Lord Fauntleroy". The outfit consisted of a velvet tunic and breeches with a lace collar.

Girls' clothes were like miniature versions of their mothers but with shorter skirts. As adult fashions changed during the Victorian era so this was reflected in their daughters' clothes. In early Victorian times girls would have worn large bonnets decorated with ribbons and flowers, dresses and long pantaloons which hung below their skirts. The sleeves of their dresses were known as leg o'mutton sleeves and would have needed a lot of material to make them puffed. Most little girls would have worn small crinolines and stiff petticoats beneath their skirts to help them stick out like their mothers'. Their dresses would have been made in two parts with a separate bodice and skirt. By the 1850s hairstyles were changing and little girls wore their hair in coiled plaits near their ears. Poke bonnets were replaced by wider brimmed hats and sleeves became bell shaped. They often carried muffs and their dresses were decorated with frills, tucks and fur trim. In the 1860s and '70s pantaloons went out of fashion and hairstyles changed again. All girls had fringes and wore their hair with an Alice band. Towards the end of the century dresses were still in two parts but as the bustle came into fashion this was incorporated as part of the bodice section lying over the skirt beneath.

Children nowadays have far less restrictive clothes without so many layers but have many more items of clothing in their wardrobes. It was usual for children to have one Sunday best outfit and only a couple of sets of clothes for the rest of the week.

Poor children

Working class children and the poor wore far simpler fashions without any of the decoration or sumptuous fabrics that wealthier children wore. Girls would wear a simple dress and pinafore and a bonnet or mob cap. Boys would wear knee length shorts with a shirt, waistcoat and cap or a simple smock. Fashion was never an issue with the poor; clothes were purchased second hand or passed down from family member to family member, repaired and patched as necessary.

Victorian women

The clothing of Victorian women was often seen as a status symbol and many husbands displayed their wealth and power through their wives' outfits. The more sumptuous the fabrics the more the class divide became apparent.

Unlike today with women's desire to lose weight and go on diets Victorian women didn't exercise or watch what they ate because fashions accommodated all shapes and sizes. Women were squeezed into tight corsets made from whalebone and then these were laced tightly to give them a small waist. Some women pulled their corsets so tight that it restricted their breathing and "swooning" was common as a result.

In the first part of Victoria's reign the crinoline was used to create a voluminous skirt. It was a stiff wire or bamboo cage which was worn over petticoats around the waist with a skirt on top. A matching bodice was worn over the corset and buttoned up at the back. Later on in the period the crinoline became smaller and was eventually replaced by the bustle. This was a pad made of fabric which fitted in the small of the back and the skirt lay over the top. This meant that the front of a dress was very flat and straight with the material gathered up at the back. Towards the end of the century all such accessories were out of fashion and long straight skirts were in vogue. Ladies' maids were necessary to help their mistresses get into and out of their clothes every day as they were difficult to do up alone. Women wore buttoned boots for daywear and these had to be done up with a buttonhook as the buttons were so tiny and fiddly. Similarly their gloves were very tight fitting and closed with buttons for which they used smaller glove hooks. These implements can be still be found in antique shops and are highly collectable.

There were certain aspects of dress which remained unchanged throughout the Victorian era. The first was that skirts never rose above the ankle and it was considered very unladylike to show your ankles unnecessarily. Hats or bonnets were always worn outside and long sleeves were always worn during daytime. Women only wore short sleeved dresses in the evening.

Victorian men

Men's clothing did not alter quite so dramatically as women's during the nineteenth century. They wore frock coats, trousers and waistcoats with a top hat when they went out. The colours of their clothes were fairly muted and a real change from fashions the in previous century. Men were far more sober and respectable and this was also reflected in the fact that most men wore beards and side-whiskers. The Victorians believed it made them look dependable and mature.

Mourning

The only significant alteration in dress came whenever the family went into mourning. If their husband died women went into deep mourning and wore black for two years out of respect. They would only leave the house to go to church or to visit close family members for the first year. For the second year it was deemed appropriate to visit the homes of close friends and in the third year they would wear whites, greys and purples. Men were only expected to wear a black armband to show mourning. Queen Victoria herself wore black for the rest of her life after Prince Albert died and she set an example which many Victorian women followed.

Clothing

LESSON PLAN

Unit 11 What was it like for children living in Victorian times?
What was life like for a poor child in the 1840s?
How did life change for children living in Victorian Britain?
- to collect information from a range of sources and draw conclusions about the Victorian period
- to understand that ways of life differed greatly across Victorian society
- to recall information about the life of children in Victorian times
- to select appropriate material and present it in a way that shows their understanding of the Victorian period

Resources

- Generic sheets 1-4

- Whiteboard or OHP

- Non-fiction texts about the Victorians which contain pictures of the rich and poor

- Envelopes

- Large sheets of paper or card

- Assorted fabrics and trimmings

- Paint, PVA glue

Starting points: whole class

Display the generic sheets one at a time on the whiteboard and ask the children to describe what the people are wearing in each one. Ask them to make assumptions about what sort of life they might have lead and give their reasons why. Compare the rich and poor children and encourage them to explain why their clothing was so different. See if they can imagine themselves dressed in the same sort of clothes as the wealthy children and ask them how they would feel going about their daily lives dressed in that way. Are there any activities they would be unable to carry out as a result of what they would be wearing? How restrictive do they think their clothes would have been?

Give them copies of the generic sheets showing the rich children and ask them to go away in groups and try to list every single item of clothing that they can see. Record this on a piece of paper which is folded in half, one half labelled 'then' and the other 'now'. Look at their own clothes and record them in the 'now' column. Once they have done this give them copies of non-fiction texts about the Victorians and ask them to research the clothing of children in order to determine what else they would have had to wear beneath their outer garments. Add these additional items to the list and them compare the two.

Keep the children in the same groups and then give them an envelope which contains one of the following written on a piece of paper, rich woman, rich man, rich boy, rich girl, poor child, working class or poor man, working class or poor woman. They need to research that particular person's dress using the internet and non-fiction texts and make notes on everything they discover as they work as a team. If you feel some of them might need a little extra help provide them with some pictures in their envelopes to help them. Once they have found out what items of dress they would wear, what sort of colours and materials they would use then ask them to draw that person on an A4 sheet of paper. Label the drawing with all the information they have gleaned so that it is fully annotated. Their next task will be to create a large collage of that person to be displayed in the classroom. It is up to you to decide if you want these to be life size or not. They will need to paint the face and body and then add material to recreate the clothes their character would have worn. Send a plea home in plenty of time to ask for scraps of material that might be suitable or visit charity shops to find velvets and satin fabrics. To make these even more impressive the children could stuff newspaper between the fabric and base sheet to give a 3D effect. They will need to keep referring to their annotated sketch in order to reproduce the clothing correctly.

Once the collages are complete the children can complete the display by creating labels and captions to add to it to explain what each article of clothing is called and any other information about it. These should be word processed to ensure consistency between all the groups.

Group activities

Activity sheet 1
This sheet is for children who need a little more support. The children need to draw a picture of themselves in what they are wearing at school on one side of the page and a picture of a Victorian child on the other side. They then need to write three similarities and differences between the clothing then and now beneath the picture.

Activity sheet 2

This sheet is for children who are more confident and work independently. The children need to draw a picture of themselves in what they are wearing at school on one side of the page and a picture of a Victorian child on the other side. They need to add labels and captions to explain the articles of dress. After that they need to list four similarities and differences between clothing then and now.

Activity sheet 3

This sheet is for the most able children. The children need to draw a picture of themselves in what they are wearing at school on one side of the page and a picture of a Victorian child on the other side. They need to add labels and captions to explain the articles of dress. After that they need to list four similarities and differences between clothing then and now. Finally they need to research the six items of clothing on the sheet and write a short sentence about each of them in their own words.

Plenary session

Show their drawings and ask them to talk about the similarities and differences between the two eras. Ask them about whether they found more similarities or differences and which set of clothes they would prefer to wear and why.

Ideas for support

For children who find some of the names of items of Victorian clothing confusing or hard to remember give them a small glossary of key items which they can refer to throughout the unit of work, for example, petticoat, pantaloons, smock, crinoline and so on. They can use this like a dictionary or as reference material. To help them they could illustrate it so they can remind themselves visually as well.

Ideas for extension

Some children will be interested in finding out more so ask them to research the changes in women's fashions that occurred during Victoria's reign. Encourage them to record the changes on a simple timeline so they can see how long each particular fashion remained in vogue.

You could ask them to write a letter to a museum or similar asking questions about the clothing of the period and telling them about what they have learned so far. Using all the information they have gleaned from their research already and what they find out from elsewhere they should create a fact file which could be displayed alongside the clothing display.

Another activity the children could carry out is to list all the different materials that the Victorians used and try to find small samples of each of them. They will need to research where these fabrics came from geographically and their origins.

Linked ICT activities

The BBC History website has a lovely section about Victorian clothing which enables the children to decide which items of clothing fit a Victorian or Tudor lady and gentleman. This will remind them of work they carried out earlier in Key Stage 2 and will enable them to see similarities and differences between the two eras. The children are shown an item of clothing and have to decide which era it belongs to. Each item correctly identified is then attached to the correct mannequin so the children can see the various layers of clothing they wore.

Find a website as a class about Victorian clothing and cut and paste a section from it into a Word document. Ask the children to edit it, add any information they wish, change the font and size of text and so on.

Rich children clothing

GENERIC SHEET

Poor children clothing

Victorian women clothing

Victorian men clothing

Children then and now

Name ....

Draw a picture of yourself here	Draw a picture of a Victorian child here

Write 3 similarities and 3 differences between the things you wear and what a Victorian child would have worn:

Similarities	**Differences**
1. _____	1. _____
2. _____	2. _____
3. _____	3. _____

Children then and now

Name ....

Draw a picture of yourself here	Draw a picture of a Victorian child here

1. Add labels and captions to your pictures to explain the items of dress.

2. List four similarities between your clothes and those of a Victorian child:

   _____   _____

   _____   _____

3. List four differences between your clothes and those of a Victorian child:

   _____   _____

   _____   _____

Children then and now

Name ....

Draw a picture of yourself here	Draw a picture of a Victorian child here

1. Add labels and captions to your pictures to explain the items of dress.

2. List four similarities between your clothes and those of a Victorian child:

_____   _____

_____   _____

3. List four differences between your clothes and those of a Victorian child:

_____   _____

_____   _____

4. Research the following items of clothing and write a short sentence about each on the back of this sheet: cravat, frock coat, drawers, crinoline, bustle, bodice.

CHAPTER 4

Education

When were schools first available?

The establishment of some schools for the poorest children was mentioned in Chapter 2 but it was not until the very end of the century that most children started going to school on a regular basis. By 1880 it became compulsory for children aged between 5 and 10 years old to attend school every day.

Education became free to everyone in 1891 which helped many families, and then in 1899 the school leaving age was raised to 12. Many families needed the wages their children could earn and school was seen as a luxury that could not be afforded before the Education Act. As in so many other aspects of Victorian life there was a huge disparity between the rich and the poor.

Many wealthy families employed governesses and tutors for their daughters to be educated at home. The boys in the family would be taught by them as well until they were old enough to be sent away. They were often sent away to boarding school aged about 8 or 9 and some attended preparatory day schools before this.

What was taught in schools?

The curriculum was much narrower in Victorian schools than it is today. There was an emphasis on the three 'Rs' – reading, writing and arithmetic. Girls were often taught needlework and all children were made fully aware of the extent of the British Empire. Children sat in rows of individual desks facing a blackboard and the teacher's desk and were often of mixed ages unlike our classes today. Schools often had two entrances, one for boys and one for girls and they would sit on opposite sides of the classroom. There would be few things on the classroom walls apart from maps and a picture of Queen Victoria. The only other items you would see would be a few books and a Bible on the teacher's desk, a globe, an abacus for maths and a cane hanging on the wall.

Corporal punishment was the norm in Victorian times. Children who misbehaved would be caned or made to wear a dunce's hat and stand facing the wall. It was thought that the children would learn by example. Children would be caned on the palm of their hands or on their bottoms. They usually received three or four strokes with "six of the best" saved for the worst transgressions.

The children wrote on slates with slate pencils and many of their lessons involved chanting and repeating what they were being taught so they learned by rote. Lessons were very didactic and there wasn't really any differentiation. The style of handwriting they taught was copperplate and the children would spend endless hours copying from the blackboard and refining their writing. When children's handwriting was sufficiently improved they were allowed to use a pen and ink. They dipped the pen into an inkwell which was part of the desk. If they made ink blots on their paper they would be punished.

Boys were thought to be more important and would be taught extra maths and science in addition to the usual curriculum. Science lessons entailed looking at an object, such as a bird's egg, or a picture of an animal, and then observe and talk about what they could see. Girls would be taught sewing and the skills needed to run a household. As well as this, moral and religious education was a vital part of their education. Children would chant moral mantras such as "cleanliness is next to godliness". "Drill" was their form of P.E. and the children would perform physical acts such as jogging, stretching and so on in unison.

What was taught in public schools?

Boys aged 12 from wealthy families would often be sent away to independent public schools which charged a fee. These schools were considered to give boys a "gentlemen's education". The best schools were Rugby, Eton, Harrow and Winchester and boys were expected to go to Oxford or Cambridge University from there. Many other schools existed but were not all of the same calibre and often boys were treated very harshly. Some schools were more interested in profit than in nurturing the boys in their care.

Younger boys were expected to do what was known as "fagging" for the senior boys which was meant to turn them into good leaders but it often led to dreadful bullying. They were expected to run errands and obey orders from the older boys with the idea that to be a good leader you had to know what it was like to be a follower.

The main subjects that were taught in public schools were Greek, Latin, history, geography and maths. None of the subjects that working class boys were taught were taught in these schools as social distinctions were observed. They were being prepared to be gentlemen rather than for a manual job. Exams were becoming important during this time. The only sports that were played at these schools were cricket and rugby as these were considered suitable for gentlemen.

Middle class boys went to day schools which were usually the grammar schools which had been set up in the Tudor and Stuart era. These schools were not of such a high standard by Victoria's reign. Preparatory schools started opening up for younger boys in order to prepare them for public school rather than going straight from a governess to boarding school.

What did governesses teach?

Wealthy families employed governesses to teach their daughters and young sons before they left for public school. Governesses were not trained teachers but were usually of good birth but whose family could not support any unmarried daughters financially. When the sons were old enough the governess would teach the remaining daughters some general knowledge, enough arithmetic to enable them to do their household accounts. Girls were expected to be able to sing, dance, play the piano, and draw a little. They learned a little French and occasionally Italian. They were taught various forms of sewing with which to while away the hours, for example, tatting, netting, wool work, plain sewing, and embroidery. One of the most important lessons girls were taught was decorum and etiquette. Many girls learned to walk across a room with a book on their head in order to teach them deportment. Not all governesses were able to teach such a range of accomplishments and sometimes masters were hired to teach their young charges. Most of these young ladies went to finishing school when they were old enough to finish their training as future wives.

Schools for girls

Schools for girls did not exist for some time, unlike those for boys. Their teachers were not usually trained either. However things changed gradually during the early part of the century and in 1848 Queen's College, London was founded as an institution to train teachers. This was followed in 1849 by Bedford College in London. In 1853 a pioneer girls' boarding school, Cheltenham Ladies' College, was founded. As time went on more schools began to open and the curriculum widened for girls and they were allowed to participate in some sports.

Sunday school

Children of all classes went to church on a Sunday. Sometimes children went twice, once in the morning and once in the evening, and they also attended Sunday school in the afternoon. They were taught about Christianity and learned passages from the Bible by heart. They were not allowed to play with any toys for the entire day unless they were overtly religious, such as a Noah's Ark.

University education

As with all other aspects of education it was considered unnecessary for women to have a good education and University was seen as the province of men. There were other universities but only Oxford or Cambridge was considered good enough for men of good family.

Towards the latter end of the century some colleges began to be opened up just for women. In 1871 Newnham College, Cambridge opened and was followed by Girton College in 1873. Oxford University followed suit and Lady Margaret Hall and Somerville accepted women. Despite this however women were not seen as valid members of the University. They were chaperoned to lectures and were not awarded degrees.

Education

Unit 11 What was it like for children living in Victorian times?
What was it like going to school at the end of the nineteenth century?
• to compare modern and Victorian schooling
• to communicate through drama their understanding of the nature of school life in Victorian times

Resources

• Generic sheet 1 – enlarge the map of the British Empire on a photocopier

• Generic sheets 2-3 – Passages written in copperplate handwriting for copying

• Globe

• Abacus

• Skipping ropes

• Hoops and sticks

• Chalk and stones for hopscotch

• Needles, thread and Binca squares

Starting points: whole class

You are going to transform your modern classroom into a Victorian classroom for a day. A few days before you start this activity send a letter home with the children asking parents if they can dress the children as Victorians for the day. In order for this to be a truly effective experience you will need to dress up yourself and mimic the way children were taught as far as possible. If you can, cover up all your displays and remove as much as possible from any surfaces in the room. You will need to arrange the tables as best you can in long rows facing the whiteboard and your own desk placed centrally. This is the best and most memorable way for the children to understand how Victorian children were educated. Depending on how your school operates it would be helpful if the children could only come into school when a bell is rung and the boys and girls enter the building through separate entrances. Try to keep this up for as much of the day as possible so the children get the full flavour of a Victorian school. You will have to explain to the children that they may not speak unless spoken to or when they are in the playground. The classroom must remain in silence unless they are being asked to speak by you or are chanting as a class.

Start your day off with registration and then some chanting of moral sayings or rules for how to behave. Remember to ask individual children to stand up and repeat them on their

own as well as whole class chanting. You should then move on to a session of handwriting demonstrating the copperplate style and asking them to copy out a passage from the whiteboard without making any mistakes. It may be helpful to provide them with copies of generic sheets 2 and 3 to help them. If you feel the children would not take it amiss "punish" some of them for sloppy writing and make them stand up with their faces to the wall or make them start all over again.

A reading session is important and you could either give the whole class a text to read aloud together or you could ask them to come up to stand beside your desk one at a time to read to you throughout the day.

For arithmetic ask the children to chant appropriate tables and number bonds and ask individual questions for the children to answer. If the children are struggling to answer give them an abacus to help them with their counting. Set some sums on the whiteboard for them to complete.

Give them a Geography lesson using a map of the British Empire which should be displayed at the front of the class along with a globe. Teach them in a really didactic way about each of the countries which make up the Empire and then ask them questions about what you have told them. Throughout the lesson get them to repeat what you are saying and ask them to come up to the front of the class and identify the countries on the globe.

At some point in the day give them an extra playtime and encourage them to play the sort of games that Victorian children would play such as skipping, hopscotch, rolling hoops with sticks, catch and tag.

If possible it would be fun to separate the boys and girls and teach the girls some simple needlework using Binca squares and the boys could do some extra maths. To make it an even more authentic experience read them passages from the Bible aloud as they sew.

Group activities

Activity sheet 1
This sheet is for children who need a little more support. They have a passage about a Victorian school to read and then highlight the most important words. Using these

highlighted words they need to write five sentences about life in a Victorian school.

Activity sheet 2

This sheet is for children who are more confident and work independently. They have a passage about a Victorian school to read and then highlight the most important words. Using these highlighted words they need to write their own passage about life in a Victorian school. Encourage them to include their own feelings and experiences of a day in a Victorian school.

Activity sheet 3

This sheet is for the most able children. They have a passage about a Victorian school to read and then highlight the most important words. Using these highlighted words they need to write their own passage about life in a Victorian school. Encourage them to include their own feelings and experiences of a day in a Victorian school. Once they have done this ask them to draw up a chart to compare the similarities and differences between modern and Victorian schools.

Plenary session

Talk with the children about their first-hand experiences in a Victorian classroom. Encourage them to share what they liked and disliked about their day. Ask children who completed the group 3 activity to share their lists of similarities and differences between Victorian and modern schooling, and discuss this as a class.

Ideas for support

Because this activity is very hands-on the children are unlikely to need as much support. Some of them may find it very difficult to conform to the behavioural requirements of the Victorian age but keep reminding them it is role play

and ensure you have classroom assistants strategically placed if necessary. There are television programmes which demonstrate a classroom in action, and the curators of local museums may be able to visit with artefacts to build up a clearer picture for the children.

Ideas for extension

Some of the children will find this experience a trigger to finding out more about Victorian childhood. Encourage them to read some of the stories written in the Victorian era, for example, Charles Kingsley's "The Water-Babies", Lewis Carroll's "Alice in Wonderland", E.Nesbit's "The Story of the Treasure Seekers", and Edward Lear's nonsense poetry.

They will have had limited experience in using some of the kinds of toys and games that Victorian children played. Give them an opportunity to research the outdoor games that Victorian children played.

Linked ICT activities

Beamish Open Air Museum has some excellent online resources that you can use with your children. There is a link which takes you to an area where you can look at a punishment book from a Victorian school. There are comprehension worksheets provided asking children to use the information from this punishment book to answer questions about one aspect of Victorian school life. There are also some photographs of Victorian schools that the children can access as well.

Ask the children to evaluate the home page and comment on the design of the buttons, icons and so on. They need to consider the use of the pictures and the text, the use of colour and ease of use.

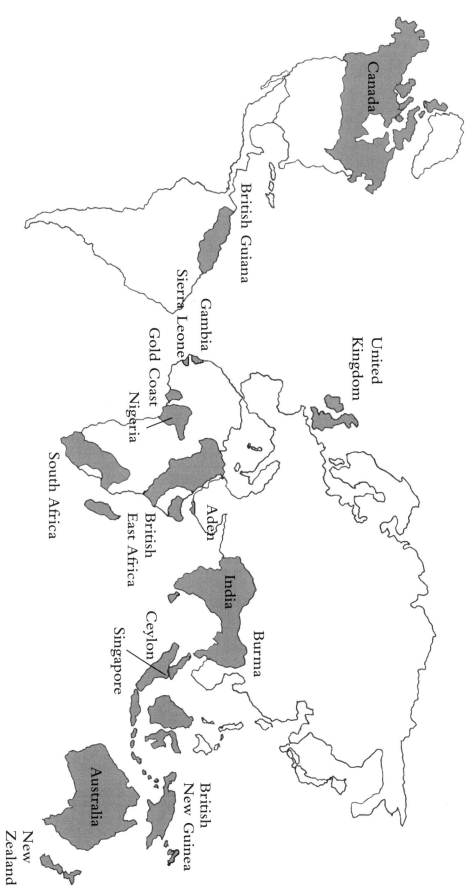

British Empire during Victoria's reign

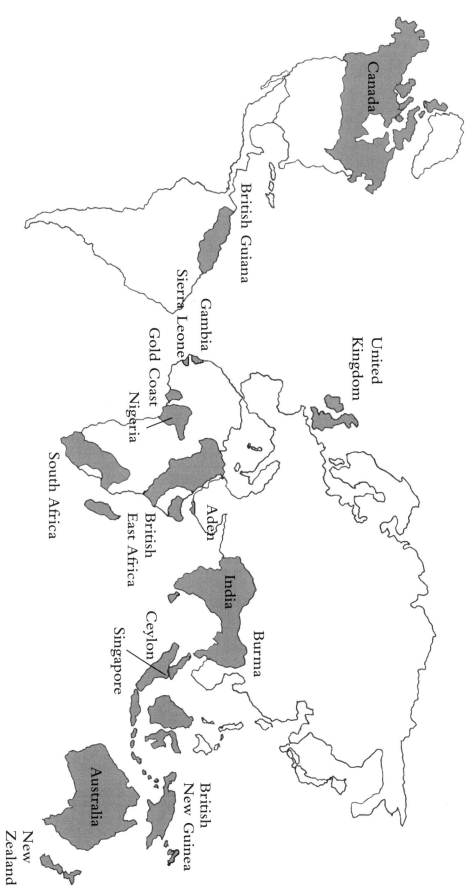

Canada

British Guiana

Gambia

Sierra Leone

Gold Coast

Nigeria

South Africa

British East Africa

Aden

United Kingdom

India

Ceylon

Singapore

Burma

Australia

New Zealand

British New Guinea

Alphabet model for handwriting practice

A B C D E F G H I
J K L M N O P Q R
S T U V W X Y Z

a b c d e f g h i j k l m n

o p q r s t u v w x y z

Alice finding a tiny door behind the curtain

Alice opened the door and found that it led into a small passage, not much larger than a rat-hole: she knelt down and looked along the passage into the loveliest garden you ever saw. How she longed to get out of that dark hall, and wander about among those beds of bright flowers and those cool fountains, but she could not even get her head though the doorway; 'and even if my head would go through,' thought poor Alice, 'it would be of very little use without my shoulders. Oh, how I wish I could shut up like a telescope! I think I could, if I only knew how to begin.' For, you see, so many out-of-the-way things had happened lately, that Alice had begun to think that very few things indeed were really impossible.

Victorian schools

Name ....

Read the passage below. Get a highlighting pen and re-read the passage. Highlight the words and phrases you think are the most important in the passage. Read the passage again to make sure you are happy with your choices.

Next, write five sentences about a typical day in a Victorian school using some of these highlighted words.

When children arrived at school the boys would go through one entrance and the girls through another. They sat at individual desks which were in rows and all faced the front of the class. The teacher's desk was in front of the blackboard and faced the children's desks.

There would be a map of the world on the wall with a picture of Queen Victoria. The only other objects in the class were a globe, a Bible, books on the teacher's desk, and a cane hanging on the wall.

Victorian teachers were very strict and if you were naughty you would be caned or made to stand at the front of the class. You were not allowed to speak in lessons unless you were told to.

Children learned their lessons by heart, they used to repeat things their teachers said and chanted spellings and tables out loud. The lessons they learned were mostly reading, writing and arithmetic. Children were taught a style of handwriting called copperplate. They wrote on slates with slate pencils until their writing was good enough. They were then allowed to use a pen which they dipped into an inkwell on their desk. If they made ink blots on their paper they would be punished.

Girls were taught sewing and how to look after a household. Boys would have extra mathematics, and some science lessons. The Victorians did not think it was important to give girls as good an education as boys, as they were being prepared to be wives and mothers.

Victorian schools

Name ....

Read the passage below. Get a highlighting pen and re-read the passage. Highlight the words and phrases you think are the most important in the passage. Read the passage again to make sure you are happy with your choices.

Next, write your own passage about a typical day in a Victorian school using these highlighted words as a starting point. You could also include your own feelings and experiences of a Victorian classroom.

When children arrived at school the boys would go through one entrance and the girls through another. They sat at individual desks which were in rows and all faced the front of the class. The teacher's desk was in front of the blackboard and faced the children's desks.

There would be a map of the world on the wall with a picture of Queen Victoria. The only other objects in the class were a globe, a Bible, books on the teacher's desk, and a cane hanging on the wall.

Victorian teachers were very strict and if you were naughty you would be caned or made to stand at the front of the class. You were not allowed to speak in lessons unless you were told to.

Children learned their lessons by heart, they used to repeat things their teachers said and chanted spellings and tables out loud. The lessons they learned were mostly reading, writing and arithmetic. Children were taught a style of handwriting called copperplate. They wrote on slates with slate pencils until their writing was good enough. They were then allowed to use a pen which they dipped into an inkwell on their desk. If they made ink blots on their paper they would be punished.

Girls were taught sewing and how to look after a household. Boys would have extra mathematics, and some science lessons. The Victorians did not think it was important to give girls as good an education as boys, as they were being prepared to be wives and mothers.

Victorian schools

Name ....

Read the passage below. Get a highlighting pen and re-read the passage. Highlight the words and phrases you think are the most important in the passage. Read the passage again to make sure you are happy with your choices.

Next, write your own passage about a typical day in a Victorian school using these highlighted words as a starting point. You should also include your own feelings and experiences of a Victorian classroom.

When children arrived at school the boys would go through one entrance and the girls through another. They sat at individual desks which were in rows and all faced the front of the class. The teacher's desk was in front of the blackboard and faced the children's desks.

There would be a map of the world on the wall with a picture of Queen Victoria. The only other objects in the class were a globe, a Bible, books on the teacher's desk, and a cane hanging on the wall.

Victorian teachers were very strict and if you were naughty you would be caned or made to stand at the front of the class. You were not allowed to speak in lessons unless you were told to.

Children learned their lessons by heart, they used to repeat things their teachers said and chanted spellings and tables out loud. The lessons they learned were mostly reading, writing and arithmetic. Children were taught a style of handwriting called copperplate. They wrote on slates with slate pencils until their writing was good enough. They were then allowed to use a pen which they dipped into an inkwell on their desk. If they made ink blots on their paper they would be punished.

Girls were taught sewing and how to look after a household. Boys would have extra mathematics, and some science lessons. The Victorians did not think it was important to give girls as good an education as boys, as they were being prepared to be wives and mothers.

Finally, draw up a table showing the similarities and differences between modern and Victorian classrooms.

5
CHAPTER

Transport

TEACHERS' NOTES

How transport changed during the Victorian era

At the beginning of the nineteenth century the principal modes of transport were by horse or on foot. Wooden sailing boats crossed the seas and oceans of the world but passengers were rarely on board. At the end of the century things were radically different. Horses were still very important and power was still measured in terms of horse power, but the railways were the most used form of transport. Cars were being used and many men were experimenting with aeroplanes and gliders.

Railways

The Victorian era was a time of great change with the Industrial Revolution and technology which changed ordinary people's lives forever. The railways were one of the greatest innovations of the time. They were highly dangerous to build and many men were killed or injured during their construction. They used dynamite to blast their way through hills and obstacles to make tunnels. The railways effectively replaced canals which had been used to transport goods and materials between major cities. The post was also collected and delivered to sorting offices by train and so post inns began to disappear on the main roads around the country. Between 1835 and 1865 25,000km of track were laid and over one hundred railway companies were formed. The most famous train of its age was George Stephenson's "Rocket" which first ran in 1829.

The first railway was built between Stockton and Darlington in County Durham in 1825. The track was 14km long and was so successful that others were being built soon after. One of the earliest tracks was between Liverpool and Manchester which gave Manchester a link to the sea, and the ability to import and export goods from Liverpool. The Manchester Ship Canal was built towards the end of the century to give the city direct access to the sea as the railway fares were expensive and the city was suffering from economic decline at the time.

The first Underground railway, the Metropolitan line, was opened in London in 1863.

The railways were originally intended for goods but gradually they began to carry passengers. In 1838 the first Great Western Railway passenger train left from Paddington station in London. It travelled at 33mph, a speed that people were wholly unused to. There were three different classes of travel but all the carriages were badly lit and were unheated. This did begin to change as the century progressed but conditions were not comfortable by modern standards. First class travel was the best as the carriages were completely enclosed and therefore sheltered the passengers. Second class carriages had solid walls up to waist level with open windows and a roof, but third class carriages were open entirely to the sky and passengers had to sit on wooden benches. The Railway Act of 1844 stated that all railway companies had to run at least one train a day which stopped at every station on a line and which cost no more than a penny a mile. It also stated that on this train all passengers had to be sheltered from the weather which improved the conditions some of the passengers endured.

Up until the birth of the railways local time was used all over the country but this had to be abolished as a fixed time had to be adhered to for the trains to run to a timetable.

With the advent of the railways came a mixture of feelings from the public. On the one hand it created new jobs. Huge gangs of "navvies" were employed to build the tracks and skilled men were employed to construct the rolling stock. Another important aspect of the growth of the railways was that people were able to travel further afield using cheap day excursion tickets. It also led to the growth of seaside resorts such as Blackpool and Weston-Super-Mare. Ordinary working class families were able to go on outings for the first time and holidays began to be taken. Journey times decreased dramatically and trade increased for some businesses. On the other hand many people were concerned about the idea of railways and there was a lot of opposition to their spread through the countryside. Many people had some of their land purchased in order to aid the spread of the routes. This upset some local people and changed the landscape of Britain. Along with the increase in jobs building the railways and rolling stock there were also job losses. Many coaching companies and inns went out of business as did many of the men who worked on the canals.

Steamships

At the beginning of the nineteenth century all ships were built of wood but were too small to trade on a large scale. After 1843 steamships made with iron, and ultimately steel, hulls were in use. During the Victorian era screw propellers, steam turbine engines and oil and diesel engines were invented and were all incorporated into the new ships. They were able to increase their speed and the distances that could be travelled as a result.

Isambard Kingdom Brunel was one of the most famous of Victorian engineers and shipbuilders. One of his boats, the "SS Great Britain", was the first with a screw propeller and was the first of its kind to cross the Atlantic in 1843. His paddle wheel boat "The Great Western" then started regular Atlantic crossings.

After 1870 Britain began to import grain from the USA, and meat from New Zealand and Argentina. This meant that people were able to have access to foods they had never been able to eat before, and it helped their household budgets. By 1900 half of the world's trade was carried in British ships.

Despite the speed of steamships, tea clippers such as the "Cutty Sark" were still faster and could carry more cargo. The "Cutty Sark" was still in use at the end of century.

Carriages

Although there were huge changes with the railways enabling people to travel longer distances horses and carriages were still needed to help people travel around. This was particularly important in rural areas. There were many different types of carriages – broughams, phaetons, governess carts, landaus, hansom cabs, and dog carts. Hackney cabs were used in London and were the taxis of their day.

Trams and Omnibuses

Trams became more widespread as the century progressed. They were predominantly horse drawn in 1861, but in 1890 electric trams on rails were being used. Omnibuses picked up numbers of passengers of all different classes and transported them around towns and cities.

Bicycles

The design of the bicycle evolved during the century. The first bicycles had seats but no pedals and you pushed yourself along by putting your feet on the ground. In 1865 the Bone-shaker or Velocipede came into being. This bicycle was the first with pedals but was very uncomfortable. It was made from wood initially but eventually had metal tyres. The Penny

Farthing was first seen in 1870 and was an all metal machine. Its unusual design with a large front wheel and tiny back wheel made it very difficult to ride and many people came off headfirst. The safety bicycle was designed after this and it was suitable for women to use. This was most like our modern bicycle and the design is essentially the same. However, it was still uncomfortable to ride and an Irishman, Mr. Dunlop, invented pneumatic tyres in 1888. He did this in order to make his son's bicycle more comfortable to ride. His invention changed the way bicycles were viewed forever.

Motor cars

By the end of the century motor cars were becoming more common. In 1863 Lenoir from Belgium invented the first car using an internal combustion engine. This was then developed by the Germans Karl Benz and Gottlieb Daimler. Another famous innovator, an American, Henry Ford, started mass production of these vehicles. The first petrol driven cars were on the roads in 1885.

Cars were viewed with suspicion and fear to begin with. The Red Flag Act of 1878 demanded a maximum speed of 4mph and in order to maintain safety a red flag was carried by someone who walked in front of the car. This continued until 1895.

Road surfaces were very poor all over the country but a man named John McAdam revolutionised road surfacing. Before his new surface was adopted roads were built using large stones which were then topped with small ones. John McAdam's idea was to cover the whole surface with small angular stones which were packed tightly together. This was called Macadamisation and by 1824 London roads were all covered in this way. In 1882 a further improvement was made by adding tar to cover the stones. This surface was called tarmacadam and is still in use today.

Transport

Unit 12 How did life change in our locality in Victorian times?
How did the arrival and expansion of the railways affect our area?
- to describe the attitudes of some different people to the building of a railway in the locality
- to communicate their understanding of benefits and disadvantages of railways
- to identify characteristic features of Victorian transport and industry

Resources

- Generic sheets 1-3

- Glue, paper, scissors

- Local maps and guidebooks

Starting points: whole class

Put the children into small groups and give them the list of Victorian modes of transport and small illustrations of each on generic sheet 1. Ask the children to cut out each picture and match them to the correct mode of transport. Once they have done this ask the children to put them in the order in which they think they were invented. They will need to discuss their choices using any knowledge they already have and make decisions as a group. Give them plenty of time to talk about the decisions they are making and come to an agreement. Stick these pictures and names onto a piece of paper in the order they choose and then come back together as a class. Show them the correct order afterwards and discuss whether they are close.

Teach the children about the different modes of transport that the Victorians used and display the pictures from generic sheets 2 and 3. It is important that the children understand the huge difference the railways made on ordinary life. People were suddenly able to travel beyond their immediate neighbourhood more easily and leisure time was spent very differently. The construction of bridges and tunnels were major feats of engineering and defied many people's expectations and changed the landscape of Britain.

As a class go to the local library or arrange a visit from a local historian who may be able to tell you about the railways in your area at that time. Talk to them about their nearest station and how they would get there nowadays. They need to find out if they are closer to or further away from a railway line than the Victorians would have been who lived in the same area. The library may well have maps and photographs of your area showing the arrival of the railway. There may also be visual clues in your town or city if you look at town maps with road names and so on.

In order to understand the contrasting attitudes towards the railways explain to the children the two different viewpoints. Their main activity will be to compare and contrast attitudes towards the railway and encourage the children to argue the case for one side or the other. Once the children have completed their activity sheet you will need to have a whole class debate with the children taking sides about the railways. Appoint a chairman and physically split the children into two sides as if it was a public meeting about the building of the railway in their town. Once everyone has had an opportunity to debate and argue their case you need to conclude the activity with a vote to see which side has been most persuasive.

Group activities

Activity sheet 1
This sheet is for children who need a little more support. There are two passages to read about the opposing views about the railways. The children will see the argument from both sides of the case. They need to list the differences between the two sides and then decide which they agree with the most. They need to write a sentence about which they favour before the class discussion takes place.

Activity sheet 2
This sheet is for children who are more confident and work independently. There are two passages to read about the opposing views about the railways. The children will see the argument from both sides of the case. They need to list the differences between the two sides and then decide which they agree with the most. Encourage them to make notes and write a sentence about which side they favour before the class discussion takes place.

Activity sheet 3
This sheet is for the most able children. There are two passages to read about the opposing views about the railways. The children will see the argument from both sides of the case. They need to write sentences highlighting the differences between the two sides and then decide which they agree with the most. They need to write a sentence about which they favour and make notes to refer to before the class discussion takes place.

Plenary session

Once the debate has concluded and they have cast their votes ask the children what difference they think the railway has made to their area if there is one nearby, or what improvements it could have made if there was one. Draw the children's attention to the fact that the same sorts of arguments and debates continue in our century over planning applications for new roads and housing. If possible link this discussion with a local issue so the children can understand how impassioned people were over the changes that were taking place in their local area.

Ideas for support

Some children will find it very hard to be able to voice an opinion in a large group so it might be helpful to work with a small group and hold a smaller version of the class debate to begin with. Use an adult to enable this to happen and give each child the opportunity to have their say.

The children could make posters to campaign for or against the railway.

Ideas for extension

Use current local maps and those from the past, if you can find any, to look for evidence of the railways. Compare and contrast the changes if there are any and ask questions as to why there is or is not a railway. They need to take into account their location, the physical geography of the area and the kinds of goods or services that were provided now and in the past.

The children could research other forms of Victorian transport and how it developed during the century.

Linked ICT activities

The Ordnance Survey website, www.ordnancesurvey.co.uk has a section entitled "Get-a-map™" and you can type in your location and postcode to find a small scale map of any area. The children could use this to search areas they have learned about in this chapter. For example they could look up Stockton and Darlington and see if they can find the original railway line. They can zoom in or out and move around using compass points to change the map of the area they want to see. This website also enables you to purchase historical maps of your area which were published in the early 1900s.

As in the previous chapter evaluate the home page of the Ordnance Survey website and compare its accessibility with that of the Beamish Open Air Museum website.

Firsts in the Victorian era

Match the pictures with the correct name. Then put these Victorian inventions in the order in which you think they were first used.

Pneumatic tyres

Paddle steamer

Internal combustion engine

Electric tram

Steam train

Petrol driven car

Penny farthing bicycle

Steam trains

Stephenson's "Rocket"

Bridges and tunnels

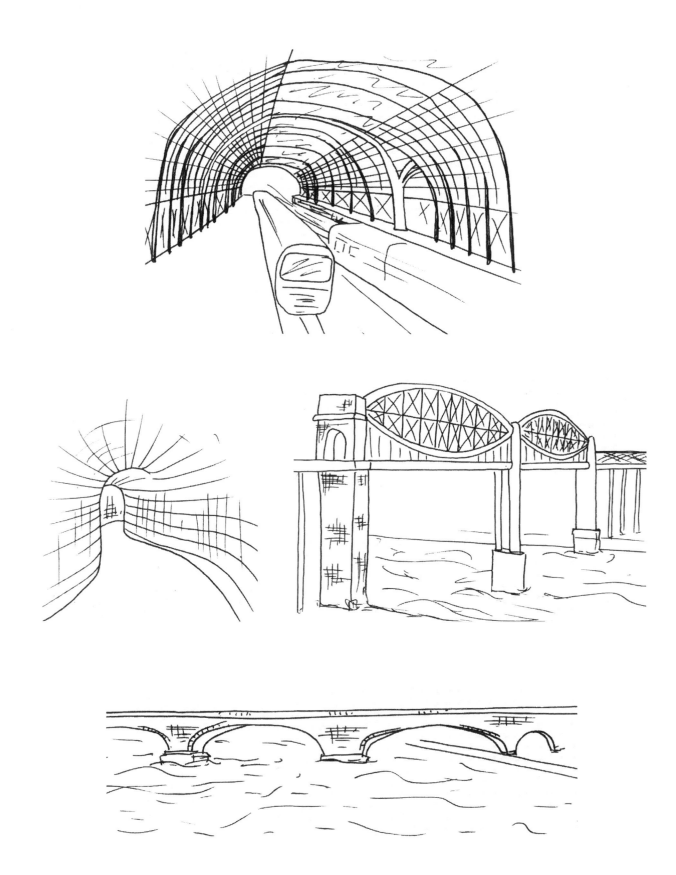

How did the Victorians feel about the railways?

Name ....

The arrival of the "iron roads" brought out a range of feelings amongst the public. Some people violently opposed them and others welcomed their arrival.

Mr Blenkinsop, factory owner

The railways are the greatest innovation of our century; our engineers are the finest men in the Empire! Progress and change! My cotton mill needs supplies and I can also send my goods much more quickly and cheaply to London and Liverpool by rail. My wife is beyond happy as her dressmaker has a wider variety of fabrics and ribbons in her shop such as you see in London. The monthly bill is costing me much less which is a great comfort to me although I do not feel she really needs a new dress and hat so often. Our family enjoyed a trip to the seaside last month and my children were delighted by the speed of the train. We were able to travel there and back in one day which surprised us all. Mr Jones has had to buy more horses and employed more ostlers to carry passengers to and from the railway station. His wife is vastly pleased as she is now able to employ an extra maid to help in their house.

Sir Edward Randall, local landowner

I am outraged at the devastation the railway is causing to the countryside around my estate. These iron monsters are breaking up the landscape and destroying the view from my drawing room window. My land and property is being defiled and the board of directors demanded I sold some of my best pastureland. The enormous viaduct they are constructing over the river is a monstrosity and the sound of explosions occurs on a regular basis. I understand from my steward that two men were badly injured last week. They will be unable to work again as their injuries are so severe. They tell me that dynamite is what they use and this fiendish fire is the cause of their distress. The London paper also reported about a gentleman of good birth who was killed when he got off a train and panicked and crossed the tracks. These terrible machines threaten to destroy all that is civilised in this great nation. Their noise and speed is terrible to behold and can only lead to devastation and despair.

Read these passages and then complete the table below listing the things which people liked and disliked about the railways.

What was good about the railways?	What was bad about the railways?
1. _____	1. _____
2. _____	2. _____
3. _____	3. _____

I agree/disagree with the railways because.................................

How did the Victorians feel about the railways?

Name ....

The arrival of the "iron roads" brought out a range of feelings amongst the public. Some people violently opposed them and others welcomed their arrival.

Mr Blenkinsop, factory owner
The railways are the greatest innovation of our century; our engineers are the finest men in the Empire! Progress and change! My cotton mill needs supplies and I can also send my goods much more quickly and cheaply to London and Liverpool by rail. My wife is beyond happy as her dressmaker has a wider variety of fabrics and ribbons in her shop such as you see in London. The monthly bill is costing me much less which is a great comfort to me although I do not feel she really needs a new dress and hat so often. Our family enjoyed a trip to the seaside last month and my children were delighted by the speed of the train. We were able to travel there and back in one day which surprised us all. Mr Jones has had to buy more horses and employed more ostlers to carry passengers to and from the railway station. His wife is vastly pleased as she is now able to employ an extra maid to help in their house.

Sir Edward Randall, local landowner
I am outraged at the devastation the railway is causing to the countryside around my estate. These iron monsters are breaking up the landscape and destroying the view from my drawing room window. My land and property is being defiled and the board of directors demanded I sold some of my best pastureland. The enormous viaduct they are constructing over the river is a monstrosity and the sound of explosions occurs on a regular basis. I understand from my steward that two men were badly injured last week. They will be unable to work again as their injuries are so severe. They tell me that dynamite is what they use and this fiendish fire is the cause of their distress. The London paper also reported about a gentleman of good birth who was killed when he got off a train and panicked and crossed the tracks. These terrible machines threaten to destroy all that is civilised in this great nation. Their noise and speed is terrible to behold and can only lead to devastation and despair.

Read these passages and then list the things which people liked and disliked about the railways using the headings below. What was good about the railways? What was bad about the railways?

Now choose which side you agree with the most ready for a class discussion and decide what sort of person you would have been in Victorian times. Make some notes about things you would like to say as that character. Complete the following sentence:

I think the railways were a good thing/a bad thing because..................................

How did the Victorians feel about the railways?

Name ....

The arrival of the "iron roads" brought out a range of feelings amongst the public. Some people violently opposed them and others welcomed their arrival.

Mr Blenkinsop, factory owner
The railways are the greatest innovation of our century; our engineers are the finest men in the Empire! Progress and change! My cotton mill needs supplies and I can also send my goods much more quickly and cheaply to London and Liverpool by rail. My wife is beyond happy as her dressmaker has a wider variety of fabrics and ribbons in her shop such as you see in London. The monthly bill is costing me much less which is a great comfort to me although I do not feel she really needs a new dress and hat so often. Our family enjoyed a trip to the seaside last month and my children were delighted by the speed of the train. We were able to travel there and back in one day which surprised us all. Mr Jones has had to buy more horses and employed more ostlers to carry passengers to and from the railway station. His wife is vastly pleased as she is now able to employ an extra maid to help in their house.

Sir Edward Randall, local landowner
I am outraged at the devastation the railway is causing to the countryside around my estate. These iron monsters are breaking up the landscape and destroying the view from my drawing room window. My land and property is being defiled and the board of directors demanded I sold some of my best pastureland. The enormous viaduct they are constructing over the river is a monstrosity and the sound of explosions occurs on a regular basis. I understand from my steward that two men were badly injured last week. They will be unable to work again as their injuries are so severe. They tell me that dynamite is what they use and this fiendish fire is the cause of their distress. The London paper also reported about a gentleman of good birth who was killed when he got off a train and panicked and crossed the tracks. These terrible machines threaten to destroy all that is civilised in this great nation. Their noise and speed is terrible to behold and can only lead to devastation and despair.

Read these passages and then write some notes using the headings listing the things which people liked and disliked about the railways. What was good about the railways? What was bad about the railways?

Now choose which side you agree with the most ready for a class discussion and decide what sort of person you would have been in Victorian times. Imagine yourself as that character and make some notes about the points you would like to use to argue your case. Complete the following sentence:

I think the railways were a good thing/a bad thing because.................................

CHAPTER 6

Inventions and the Industrial Revolution

What was the Industrial Revolution?

Although the Industrial Revolution characterised the Victorian era it actually began during the second half of the eighteenth century. There were many great innovators and inventors who initiated many of the dramatic changes which changed people's lives in the nineteenth century. With the numerous engineering feats and inventions that were taking place industry became mechanised and changed the face of Britain. There was a large migration of workers from rural areas to major towns and cities swelling their population dramatically. Many men prospered from their new businesses and the "middle classes" were formed. People who worked and earned their wealth now had access to the privileges of the rich and their children had opportunities available to them that their parents had missed.

During the nineteenth century Britain became known as the "workshop of the world", primarily because by 1870 more than one third of the world's manufactured goods came from this country. By 1900 75% of the steamships in the world were built in Britain and many key innovations took place here.

However, despite the wealth and power that came with all these changes there was a negative side. Working conditions were poor for the vast majority of factory workers and there was terrible poverty. For those who were out of work life was incredibly hard and many families ended up in the workhouse as they were unable to support themselves. Living conditions were often poor even for those who were working and many people had to send their children out to work in order to be able to keep food on the table and a roof over their heads.

Industrial change

The textile industry arguably changed the most during the Victorian era. Richard Arkwright's Spinning Jenny and Samuel Crompton's Spinning Mule in the eighteenth century started the changes to this industry. By the beginning of the nineteenth century mechanised cotton mills were appearing all over the north of England and made many men very wealthy. Weaving had essentially been a cottage industry before this and predominantly only used wool. The various different stages of the process were carried out at different locations where the skills lay. As machines began to take over from manpower all the different strands of the weaving process were brought under one roof and horse power was used to power the machines.

This gave way to water power and ultimately steam. Wool was no longer the most common material; cotton and flax were imported and processed through the factories. It was a huge industry which employed hundreds of people in one location. It was noisy and dangerous and safety became a big issue as the century progressed.

As was mentioned in the previous chapter the dawn of steam power changed the way people travelled and transported manufactured goods. Steam not only powered the railways but also machinery in mines and factories. Tin mining was at the forefront of industry in Cornwall and this was mainly because of an invention in the early 1800s by Richard Trevithick. He developed a high pressure steam engine to drain the shafts of water to prevent flooding.

Iron foundries no longer used charcoal for powering the furnaces. Coke was used instead so the mining industry boomed at the same time. Coal shafts were dug far deeper than in the past because steam engines were able to pump out water from them. It was a hazardous existence and there were many terrible accidents with miners trapped underground because of rock falls and mechanical failures.

Innovators of the Industrial Revolution

There were innumerable inventors and engineers during the Victorian era but the most important are household names, some of them without us realising. For example, James Watt (1736-1819) developed the use of steam power to drive factory machinery and the watt, a unit of electric power was named after him. Thomas Telford (1757-1834) was a major road engineer, and he also built homes, prisons, bridges and the Ellesmere Canal which linked Wales to the River Mersey. He also built the road from London to Holyhead where people could then take a ferry to Ireland. The Menai Straits suspension bridge is another of his successes.

George Stephenson (1781-1848) was mentioned in the previous chapter and he built steam locomotives and railway lines and was known as 'the father of the railways'. Another name that has already appeared is that of Isambard Kingdom Brunel (1806-1859). He was the engineer who liked to tackle a solution to a big problem, such as building a tunnel beneath the River Thames.

Two other important names were Louis Daguerre (1781-1851) and William Armstrong (1810-1900). Daguerre invented the first practical camera which was known as the

Daguerrotype. He coated a plate with silver iodide to capture pictures of people and places from 1840 onwards. The only problem with his invention was that you could only have one copy of each picture. It is thanks to his experimenting that we have photographs of life in the Victorian era. Armstrong was a solicitor who started an engineering firm having been fascinated by the power of water while he was fishing. He harnessed water power to provide electric power and heating for his house. He was not only famous for his hydraulic engineering abilities but he also invented an early form of artillery gun known as the Armstrong gun.

Trade Unions

It was during the Victorian era that trade unions began. They came about as a direct result of the changes brought by the Industrial Revolution. As more and more people worked in factories they began to realise that working conditions were not good enough. Men grouped together to form trade unions in order to improve working conditions and pay for all. Some trade unions were even able to give sickness and unemployment pay. By the end of the century about a quarter of all workers were in a union. These groups of men used to meet in pubs when they first began and many pubs were named after them as a result, for example, the Bricklayers Arms. Robert Owen (1771-1858) was a very important proponent of the trade unions and the co-operative movement. He fought hard to improve conditions for factory workers. He was in an ideal position to appreciate the needs of the workers as he was in charge of a mill himself. He improved the lot of his own workers and also set up a school for their children.

The Co-operative Movement

The Co-operative Movement was started by 28 weavers who opened a grocery shop in Rochdale in 1844. Similar shops were opened subsequently. They sold good quality food, clothes and other goods at reasonable prices. Members were also able to join a savings scheme through the co-operative. This was a real departure as many factory owners had their own shops and paid their workers in tokens that could only be spent in their shop. The produce was not of such good quality and was more expensive than that of the co-operatives so this was a real step forwards.

The initial co-operative worked in the following way, each of the weavers put in one pound to begin with to buy oatmeal, sugar, candles and other household goods. These items were then sold to customers for a fair price unlike the factory owners' shops. Each customer received a dividend which varied according to how much they bought at the shop and any end of year profits were divided between them. These profits could either be spent in the shop or left in the business as a form of investment. The Co-operative still continues these days but has expanded and diversified.

Victorian inventions

The Industrial Revolution was not just about factories, railways and feats of engineering, there were many other smaller inventions. These may appear to be insignificant alongside some of the more obvious changes but they have all had a major impact on people's lives then and now. These inventions were the forerunner to the modern technology we use today. The first typewriter was used in 1851.

The first sewing machine was invented in 1886 which made a real difference to the clothing industry and mass-produced clothing was manufactured. Women were expected to be able to sew their own family's clothes and although needlework was still an important skill it began to be less essential. The first wireless was available in 1899 and the first gramophones in 1897 so people were able to hear music in their own homes.

Another common household item was invented in 1878 and until recently its design remained relatively unchanged. The electric light bulb was a radical departure from candlelight or oil lamps which had been used until then. In London the first public lavatories were unveiled and people could use these at the cost of one penny, and subsequently the phrase "spending a penny" became common.

Alexander Graham Bell invented the first telephone in 1875 and Marconi was involved in developing the system to send the first wireless telegraphic messages across the Atlantic.

Inventions and the Industrial Revolution

Unit 12 How did life change in our locality in Victorian times?
Who lived here in 1841?
Who lived and worked here in 1891? What has changed since 1841 and why?
• to make comparisons that illustrate change within the Victorian period
• to give reasons for these changes
• to identify characteristic features of Victorian transport and industry

Resources

• Generic sheets 1–3

• Copies of local census forms

Starting points: whole class

Teach the children about what the Industrial Revolution entailed and how life changed for working class people in terms of the work they had to carry out. Introduce them to some of the principal innovators of the time and the industrial change that they brought about. Discuss some of the major inventions of the time and how they have been adapted over time. How many of these inventions are still in use on a daily basis in their own homes?

The History section of the Standards Site has some valuable activities using census returns for 1841 and 1891 to illustrate to the children the changes that occurred in their area as a result of the Industrial Revolution. By looking at local census returns they will be able to see how the population grew in their area and the changes in people's job titles. There may well be other clues from street names which will give them an idea of the radical changes that swept across the country. If possible find an old street map of your locality through the local library and compare it with a current map. You will need to take the children out to visit their closest town to look for evidence of Victorian industry. If you are fortunate enough you will be able to take them to a working museum to demonstrate first hand the sort of environment people had to work in. This lesson plan will consolidate this work and enhance what the children observe.

Show the children the information about a small section of the population of a town on generic sheet 1. Read it through with the children and ask them to comment on the number of people in one household, their ages and occupations and so on. Discuss whether or not this fictional town is similar in any way to their locality at the same time. It may be of interest to use local sources of information to find out how the population changed in your area between 1841 and 1891. The national population of England and Wales doubled during Victoria's reign, from 15,914,000 in 1841 to 32,528,000 in 1901.

The activity sheets ask the children to add information to a sample census form which is partially complete. This information is all contained within generic sheet 1 so the children need to read it thoroughly and check with the census to see where there are gaps. Each activity sheet then asks questions for the children to answer from the census form. Some of the questions ask the children to make inferences based on the knowledge they already have and the information on the census.

Group activities

Activity sheet 1
This sheet is for children who need a little more support. The question sheet asks the children to look for answers which they can lift directly from the sample census. They will need to look carefully at the census and use the headings to help them find their answers.

Activity sheet 2
This sheet is for children who are more confident and work independently. The question sheet asks the children to look for answers which they can lift directly from the sample census. There are also a couple of questions which they will need to answer through making inferences using the information in front of them.

Activity sheet 3
This sheet is for the most able children. The question sheet asks the children to look for answers which they can lift directly from the sample census. There are also a number of questions which they will need to answer through making inferences using the information in the census. The children also need to make up a family of their own for 7, Railway Cottages. This family also work in the cotton mill so their writing should reflect this.

Plenary session

Show the children the complete census on Generic sheet 3 and ask the children to compare their own forms with this. Ask the children if they think Ethel Jarvis' deafness would have made a difference to her work in the cotton mill. Tell the children that these cottages would have had two bedrooms at the most. Look at the census again and ask the children if they can work out how each family would fit into these small homes.

Ideas for support

If possible find some photographs or borrow artefacts from a local museum to show the children some of the inventions of the Victorian age. The children can sketch these and compare them with modern versions of the same machine.

Ideas for extension

The children could choose one of the Victorian inventors and research their lives and work. This could be presented like a fact file and displayed in the classroom.

Another way this work could be extended is to ask the children to write a diary entry imagining themselves as a child who worked in a cotton mill. This could be about their working day as well as life in a large family in a small house.

Linked ICT activities

There are some excellent ICT resources which can be used to back up this unit of work. There is an interesting

animated story about James Watt and an explanation about his steam engine using Espresso. The Beamish Open Air Museum in County Durham has a very interesting website with some good resources which will enhance this work. There are some fascinating photos of mining in Victorian times. These can be pasted into a Word document and the children can type some sentences to explain what is going on in the picture. Another section of the website has resources about George Stephenson with interactive whiteboard sheets, worksheets, and so on which you can use to enhance this unit of work.

To initiate this work ask the children to type in the URL to locate each of these web pages. Once they have found out some interesting facts ask the children to select one of these inventors or an aspect of industry and use a search engine to do some further research.

Families in Railway Cottages, Ormsdale, Lancashire, 1851

The Jarvis family lived at number 1, Railway Cottages. There were three children, Betsy, 12, William, 10 and Ethel, 6. Their parents, Robert and Charlotte worked in the cotton mill and both were weavers. All the children worked in the mill for half a day every day and went to school for the other half. The two oldest children were piecers and Ethel was a scavenger.

The Wingfield family lived at number 3, Railway Cottages. There were 5 children in this family aged 6 months, 2, 6, 7 and 9. Two of the children were mill workers, the oldest being a piecer. Their father George was a fly maker and his wife was a weaver. Her mother lived with them and she was a lace maker.

The Millers were the smallest family on the street at number 5, Railway Cottages. The youngest son, Edward, was 17 and he was a spinner. His sister Elsie was a bobbin carrier. The eldest son was 24 and was a weaver. Their mother worked on the carding floor.

No. of house-holder schedule	Name of street, place, or road, and name, or no. of house	Name and surname of each person who abode in the house, on the night of the 30th March, 1851	Relation to Head of family	Condition	Age of males	Age of females	Rank, profession, or occupation	Where born	Whether blind, or deaf and dumb
117	1, Railway Cottages		Head	Married	34		Weaver	Ormsdale, Lancs	
		Charlotte Jarvis	Wife	Married		33		D°	
		Betsy Jarvis	Daughter			12	Piecer	D°	
		William Jarvis	Son		10			D°	
		Ethel Jarvis	Daughter			6		D°	Deaf
118	3, Railway Cottages		Head	Married	45		Fly maker	Ribble Valley, Lancs	
		Eliza Wingfield	Wife	Married		34	Weaver	Bolton, Lancs	
		Eleanor Dearden	Mother-in-law	Widow		61		Sheffield, Yorks	
		Thomas Wingfield	Son				Piecer	Ormsdale, Lancs	
		James Wingfield	Son		7		---	D°	
		Emily Wingfield	Daughter			6	Scavenger	D°	
		Matthew Wingfield	Son		2			D°	
		Kate Wingfield	Daughter			6 months		D°	
119	5, Railway Cottages	Charles Miller	Head	Single			Weaver	Ormsdale, Lancs	
		Harriet Miller	Mother	Widow		42	Carder	Ireland	
		Edward Miller	Son	Single	17		Bobbin carrier	Ormsdale, Lancs	
			Daughter			14		D°	

No. of house-holder schedule	Name of street, place, or road, and name, or no. of house	Name and surname of each person who abode in the house, on the night of the 30th March, 1851	Relation to Head of Family	Condition	Age of males	Age of females	Rank, profession, or occupation	Where born	Whether blind, or deaf and dumb
117	1, Railway Cottages	Robert Jarvis	Head	Married	34		Weaver	Ormsdale, Lancs	
		Charlotte Jarvis	Wife	Married		33	Weaver	D°	
		Betsy Jarvis	Daughter			12	Piecer	D°	
		William Jarvis	Son		10		Piecer	D°	
		Ethel Jarvis	Daughter			6	Scavenger	D°	Deaf
118	3, Railway Cottages	George Wingfield	Head	Married	45		Fly maker	Ribble Valley, Lancs	
		Eliza Wingfield	Wife	Married		34	Weaver	Bolton, Lancs	
		Eleanor Dearden	Mother-in-law	Widow		61	Lace maker	Sheffield, Yorks	
		Thomas Wingfield	Son		9		Piecer	Ormsdale, Lancs	
		James Wingfield	Son		7		D°	D°	
		Emily Wingfield	Daughter			6	Scavenger	D°	
		Matthew Wingfield	Son		2			D°	
		Kate Wingfield	Daughter			6 months		D°	
119	5, Railway Cottages	Charles Miller	Head	Single	24		Weaver	Ormsdale, Lancs	
		Harriet Miller	Mother	Widow		42	Carder	Ireland	
		Edward Miller	Son	Single	17		Spinner	Ormsdale, Lancs	
		Elsie Miller	Daughter			14	Bobbin carrier	D°	

Railway Cottages census activity

Name ....

Use the census and information sheet to answer these questions in full sentences.

1. Read Generic sheet 1 which tells you about the people who lived in Railway Cottages. Now fill in the missing details on Generic sheet 2 using this information.

2. How many people lived at 3, Railway Cottages? How many of these were children?

   _____

3. Find out what each of these jobs involved in a cotton mill and briefly explain them:

   • Bobbin carrier _____

   • Carder _____

   • Piecer _____

   • Scavenger _____

   • Spinner _____

   • Weaver _____

4. How many residents were weavers and what were their names? _____

   _____

5. How many children under the age of 12 worked in the cotton mill? _____

6. Which family had three generations living under the same roof? _____

   _____

Railway Cottages census activity

Name ....

Use the census and information sheet to answer these questions in full sentences.

1. Read Generic sheet 1 which tells you about the people who lived in Railway Cottages. Now fill in the missing details on Generic sheet 2 using this information.

2. How many people lived at 3, Railway Cottages? How many of these were children?

   _____

3. Find out what each of these jobs involved in a cotton mill and briefly explain them:

   • Bobbin carrier _____

   • Carder _____

   • Piecer _____

   • Scavenger _____

   • Spinner _____

   • Weaver _____

4. How many residents were weavers and what were their names?

   _____

5. Which jobs did children under the age of 12 do in the cotton mill?

   _____

6. Which family had three generations living under the same roof?

   _____

7. Look at the Miller family's entries. Why do you think Charles Miller was the head of the family?

   _____

Railway Cottages
census activity

Name ....

Use the census and information sheet to answer these questions in full sentences.

1. Read Generic sheet 1 which tells you about the people who lived in Railway Cottages. Now fill in the missing details on Generic sheet 2 using this information.

2. How many people lived at 3, Railway Cottages? How many of these were children?

3. Find out what each of these jobs involved in a cotton mill and briefly explain them: Bobbin carrier, Carder, Piecer, Scavenger, Spinner, Weaver

4. How many residents were weavers and what were their names?

5. How many children under the age of 12 worked in the cotton mill?

6. Which jobs did these children do and does their age make a difference to the job they do?

7. Which family had three generations living under the same roof?

8. Look at the Miller family's entries. Why do you think Charles Miller was the head of the family?

9. Why do you think James Wingfield was not working in the cotton mill like the other older children?

10. If George and Eliza Wingfield were both working who do you think looked after their youngest children for them? Why do you think it is this person?

11. Now make up another family who live at 7, Railway Cottages. They also worked in the cotton mill so the information you give should reflect this.

CHAPTER 7

Rich and poor

Slums

After the Industrial Revolution there were many more people living in the towns and cities of Britain. There was a mass migration of workers from the countryside where many of them could not find work any more. The very machinery that gave them jobs in factories had put them out of work on the land as labour was mechanised. As a result of these population explosions around the country housing became overcrowded and many people were reduced to penury if they could not find work. The housing that was available became overcrowded and slums were common in all cities. Many families lived in cramped and insanitary conditions often sharing just one tap and toilet per 25 families. People worked to survive and even then they were often starving and desperate.

Children were sent out to work to supplement the family income working in factories, young boys as chimney sweeps, and for those less fortunate selling goods on the streets. Match girls were a common sight, and children were paid for rat catching and "mudlarking" beside the River Thames looking for things to sell. Some children even bought food scraps and used tea leaves from the kitchens of the well-to-do and sold them on to poorer people. Another thankless job was known as a "pure finder" who collected dogs' faeces and sold it to tanneries where it was used to darken hides. To imagine children carrying out such jobs in order to eat seems unthinkable to us but the disparity between rich and poor was very great and living conditions were incredibly hard.

Many people who lived in the slums ended up turning to crime in order to support their families. We are all familiar with Dickens' story "Oliver Twist" which tells us of the orphan boys who were trained as pickpockets. Walking the streets could be dangerous for both rich and poor alike.

The Workhouse

The Workhouse is not unfamiliar to anyone, of all Victorian innovations it is perhaps the most infamous. In 1834 the government passed the Poor Law Amendment Act which said that all people seeking poor relief, orphans, the sick, the old and the unemployed would go into a workhouse. There would be no poor relief in any other form. Many people saw this as a solution to a growing problem and that workhouse life might be a deterrent for asking for such help. Inmates were given food and clothing but were expected to work very hard and follow the very strict rules that were laid down. When families entered the workhouse they were split up, as were men and women. For many

people who were entering the workhouse as a last resort this was a terrible thing to happen to them and many families did their utmost to avoid this situation. There were seven classes of inmates, aged and infirm men, able bodied men and youths over 13, youths and boys over the age of seven and under 13, aged or infirm women, able bodied women and girls over 16, girls above 7 years old and under 16, and finally children under 7 years of age. Charles Dickens' feelings about the workhouse are evident when you read his novel "Oliver Twist". They may well be an imagined extreme but it is not beyond the bounds of possibility that many workhouses were that bad.

Life as a poor child

For the fortunate families who were able to keep themselves out of the workhouse life was a daily struggle. The Victorians had large families so there was less food to go round. Infant mortality rates were very high but without contraception families grew rapidly. Children were sent to work as soon as they were old enough in order to supplement the income brought in by their parents. Many children were hungry, cold, and neglected by modern standards on a regular basis. Small boys were employed as chimney sweeps and had to climb chimneys to clean for the master sweep. In 1847 the "Ten Hours" Act limited working time to ten hours for children; to modern children who are only at school for six and a half hours a day this seems inconceivable. By 1880 all children had to attend school although many worked afterwards. Our six week summer holiday also has its origins in the past where children were needed to help to bring in the harvest and many children would not be able to attend school at that time of year.

Poor children did not have changes of clothes and many of them went barefoot more often than not. Toys were minimal and were often made from whatever was to hand; proper toys were for the rich and beyond the means of the poor.

Nursery life

For children with rich parents their lives were comfortable and cosseted. There would be a nurse who was the principal carer for the young children. Their parents would rarely see their children, and when they were allowed in with papa and mama they were expected to be 'seen and not heard'.

The daily routine of the children was the same every day but Sunday. The children would have breakfast, and then go for a walk in the park. They would then return home where the children would play and have lessons. After this they would have lunch, followed by a rest. They would then have time to play followed by tea time. After this they would change their clothes and then go to visit mama downstairs. In the parlour they would recite poems, sing songs, talk and play. After a little while they would return to the nursery for bath and bedtime. Children often had more love and affection bestowed on them by their nurses than their parents. Children in such families often had pet dogs and there would always be plenty of toys, such as, dolls, toy soldiers, musical boxes, board games, train sets, dolls' houses, and rocking horses. Teddy bears were not in existence until 1902 after an incident with the U.S. President Theodore Roosevelt during a bear hunting trip.

Boys were educated to become young gentlemen and have a place in the world of work whereas girls were prepared for marriage.

London life for the rich

Living in London as a rich child was radically different from a child living in the slums in the East End. London was divided into areas of wealth and poverty and many areas were considered 'no go' areas for people of a certain class. The upper and middle classes had streets lit by gas light and many of the wealthier families used gas light in their homes as well. Some areas of housing were in private roads with gatekeepers who allowed people in and out. Some houses had mews behind for their horses and carriages. These houses often had several floors with the servants quarters in the garrets and the nursery just below. Servants were "owned" by their master and mistress. They went to bed after their master and rose before him in order to prepare breakfast and lay the fires. They did not have a day off and were expected to attend church on Sundays with the family. Some servants were allowed a week to visit their own family once a year and occasionally some had a half day holiday a week. Despite their lot in life many servants felt blessed to be in a position of security rather than living a life of poverty elsewhere.

The rich had baths every day and access to all the modern conveniences of the Victorian age. They had evenings out to dinner parties, the theatre, balls and so on and rarely had to concern themselves over the welfare of anyone but themselves. The class divide was so great that many wealthy people were unaware of the terrible poverty that was so close to them. It was only a few whose consciences allowed them to see the disparity and help those in need.

Rich and poor

Unit 11 What was it like for children living in Victorian times?

What was life like for a poor child in the 1840s?
How did life change for children living in Victorian Britain?
• to collect information from a range of sources and draw conclusions about the Victorian period
• to understand that ways of life differed greatly across Victorian society
• to write a narrative using historical detail
• to understand that there are many representations of the Victorian period
• to recall information about the life of children in Victorian times
• to select appropriate material and present it in a way that shows their understanding of the Victorian period

Resources

• Generic sheets 1-2

• A copy of Charles Dickens' "Oliver Twist"

• A copy of Charles Kingsley's "The Water-Babies"

• Non-fiction texts about the Victorians

• Large sheets of paper

Starting points: whole class

To start off this unit of work read the children some passages from "Oliver Twist" so they can listen to a recount of life in a workhouse. Encourage the children to share their reactions to this and ask them what they already know about workhouses. Once they have had plenty of opportunities to discuss what they have heard and related it to any prior knowledge show the children pictures of rich and poor children from the Victorian era using generic sheet 1. Ask them to identify the differences between the two sets of children and make a list of them under the headings "Rich" and "Poor". Discuss the differences and ask the children if they have seen children in such reduced circumstances before. They may have seen pictures of children in the Third World who live in poverty and are aware of the hardships they face. Compare these situations and ask them if there is any difference between now and then.

Teach the children about the life lead by rich children in those days and that of a poor child. Talk with them about which of the children had the most freedom and independence. Ask them questions such as which of these children had the most opportunities available to them? Which children had a family life most like ours? Which aspects of a poor child's life do you think a rich child would benefit from and vice versa?

If you are able to watch a television programme about the lives of Victorian children it would be really helpful. You could show them clips from an adaptation of "Oliver Twist" showing his life with Mr. Brown in luxury and his life in the workhouse. This might give the children a better picture of the huge disparity between the rich and poor. The story "The Water Babies" by Charles Kingsley is about a little chimney sweep called Tom. The first chapter gives an excellent illustration of the life of a small boy working for a cruel master and the difference between his life and that of Ellie who lives in the big house. Read this to the children and ask them to consider the difference between their lives and those of children like Tom.

Give the children plenty of non-fiction books about Victorian life and ask the children to use the contents and index pages to find information about life as a Victorian child. Provide each group with a large sheet of paper divided into two and labelled rich and poor. As a group read through the texts and find as much information as possible about childhood and record it in the relevant area as notes. Allow them plenty of time to do this and use as many sources as possible including any ICT resources you may have. Once all the groups have found out as much as they can ask the children to share some of the things they have learned.

The activity sheets ask the children to draw a "comic strip" of a day in the life of a poor child in 1840 and then to write a narrative about the activities they carry out and how they feel. Encourage them to think about whether the child is working or not, how old they are and the responsibilities they have at home.

Group activities

Activity sheet 1
This sheet is for children who need a little more support. The children need to use the research they have carried out to draw four separate activities that a poor child would carry out in their daily life. They need to write a sentence below each picture explaining what the child is doing.

Activity sheet 2

This sheet is for children who are more confident and work independently. The children need to use the research they have carried out to draw six separate activities that a poor child would carry out in their daily life. They need to write some sentences below each picture explaining what the child is doing.

Activity sheet 3

This sheet is for the most able children. The children need to use the research they have carried out to draw six separate activities that a poor child would carry out in their daily life. They then need to write a personal narrative describing their life as a poor child.

Plenary session

Encourage the children to share their writing and see if they can empathise with the child they are writing about. Ask them to think about the things they may not like in their life, getting up to go to school, homework and so on and decide whether their lives are preferable to that of a child in the 1840s. Ensure they give you a reason why they feel a certain way.

Ideas for support

In order to develop their research skills ensure there is an adult to help and guide them as they use the texts to search for information on Victorian childhood. Reinforce how to use the contents and index pages of books to find information, giving them an alphabetical strip to help them locate the letters of the alphabet.

If the children are having trouble establishing what a poor child in the 1840s would do on a normal day then insert pictures in the spaces on the activity sheets and ask then to write about those. You could put in a selection of different aspects of life and work instead of limiting them to one particular child.

Ideas for extension

Once the children have written an account of their day as a poor child you could encourage them to do the same for a rich child. They could also investigate the role of a governess, a nurse and the other servants in the homes of the wealthy. They could dramatise some of their accounts and present them to the rest of the class.

The children could also extend their comprehension of the living conditions of the poor by writing a newspaper article about the slums and trying to exhort the authorities to do something about improving conditions for the inhabitants. Another thing you could ask the children to do is to research workhouses thoroughly and then write some rules for an imaginary workhouse in their town.

Linked ICT activities

The BBC website has another section on its Victorian Britain site entitled "Rich and Poor Families" which has some interesting photographs and facts for the children to look at. Within this section there are some short videos for the children to watch and there is an interesting one about the role of a governess, and about children from the workhouse working as apprentices in a textile mill. The website "Virtual Victorians" also allows the children to look at what a family who worked in a factory did each day of the week.

Once again the children are going to create their own document. On a page you create write a few sentences about each of these websites with their hyperlinks. Use these hyperlinks to navigate a page and find information. When they have done this teach the children to save and use pictures and text and import them into a document for a presentation.

Rich and poor Victorian children

Rich and poor
Victorian children

Life as a poor child in 1840

Name ....

In each of the boxes draw an activity that a poor child in 1840 would carry out every day. Write a sentence for each activity explaining what the child is doing.

Life as a poor child in 1840

Name ....

Imagine that you are a poor child in 1840. In each of the boxes draw an activity that you would carry out every day. Cut out each picture stick it on a page and write some sentences for each activity explaining what you are doing.

Life as a poor child in 1840

Name ....

Imagine that you are a poor child in 1840. In each of the boxes draw an activity that you would carry out every day. Write a narrative explaining a day in your life using the research you have carried out.

Sports and leisure

CHAPTER 8

TEACHERS' NOTES

Until the Victorian era sport and leisure time was the preserve of the rich. During this time it became more normal for working and lower class Victorians to have leisure time. Up until the middle of the century the working classes worked a six day week. The term "the weekend" was used from 1870 as people were slowly allowed to work for only the five days of the week. The Victorians started going on trips to the seaside and the countryside. For those who could not afford to travel they would visit local parks and zoos. It also gradually became respectable for women to play sports.

Cricket, Football and Boxing

Cricket, football and boxing were already in existence but during the Victorian era the rules were formalised and adopted all over the country. Some of the football clubs that are in existence now were set up by churches. Everton and Aston Villa are examples of such clubs. They did this in order to increase their congregation size. Other clubs were set up by employers in order to improve industrial relations between workers and managers. Arsenal and Manchester United are examples of clubs set up for the workers. Additional rules were added as the century progressed as there was too much foul play taking place. Free kicks were introduced in 1877 and penalty kicks in 1891. The first F.A. Cup competition took place in 1871.

The Marylebone Cricket Club (the MCC) was started in 1787 by a group of wealthy men. The County Championship began in 1873 and nine English counties qualified. Gloucestershire dominated the competition for a long time. This was mainly due to the legendary cricketer W.G. Grace and his two brothers who played on the team.

English cricketers travelled to Australia in 1861 for the first time to play against their national team. In 1882 the Australians played a Test match in England and our cricketers lost. The following was published in The Sporting Times, "*In affectionate remembrance of English cricket which died at the Oval on 29th August, 1882. Deeply lamented by a large circle of sorrowing friends and acquaintances. R.I.P. N.B. The body will be cremated and the ashes taken to Australia.*" It is believed that the bails were burned and the ashes placed in a small urn. It is these ashes that the two teams still play for biennially.

Boxing was a sport that was often played in the background and was not considered legitimate until the twentieth century. Fights often happened in areas where gambling took place and were often stopped by the police. Modern boxers still play by the rules laid down in 1867 by the Marquess of Queensbury.

Tennis

In 1837 Major Walter Wingfield invented a game called Sphairistike. As time went on the rules were formalised and the name was changed to Lawn Tennis. Tennis became more fashionable as the century progressed but it was in the 1870s when it was at its most popular with men and women. Changes in fashion allowed women to play although by modern standards their clothing was very cumbersome. The All England Croquet club in Wimbledon handed one bowling lawn to this new sport and the first championship was held there in 1877. The rest is history and Wimbledon is now one of the major Grand Slam tournaments for professional players.

Rugby

The modern game of rugby supposedly came into existence in 1823 at the school Rugby. Boys at Rugby had played football from 1750 but boys were allowed to handle the ball. It is said that William Webb Ellis took a ball in his arms and ran with it and so the sport was born. The boys at the school formalised their rules in 1870 and they were adopted all over the world. The headmaster at the time, Dr. Thomas Arnold, was very keen on promoting a balance of sport and academic work and this began to be adopted by other boarding schools in the country.

Music Hall

The music hall was a very popular aspect of Victorian life. Both rich and poor attended but it was considered inappropriate for women and children. Acrobats, magicians, singers, dancers and so on entertained the masses night after night in a set of variety acts. Many well-known songs emerged from this era such as "Any Old Iron", "Champagne Charlie", "I Do Like to Be Beside the Seaside" and "My old Man (Said Follow the Van)".

Girls at home

The sorts of toys that children played with at this time were mentioned in Chapter 7. Whilst older boys were away at school the older girls were left at home. They were expected to entertain themselves by developing their accomplishments. They were expected to read, embroider, make objects with shells and wax, sketch, play the piano, sing, and read aloud.

Pantomime

Many modern children find it hard to imagine how Victorian children entertained themselves. In a world without electronic gadgets and television one of the highlights of a child's year was the annual pantomime. Traditionally pantomimes opened on Boxing Day and children would go on a family outing over the Christmas period. Pantomimes were similar to modern versions as they included songs, dances and jokes. Unlike modern pantomimes there was always a closing Harlequinade. This was originally the main part of the performance and it would feature a Columbine, a Harlequin, a Pantaloon and a Clown.

Garden parties

Victorians were very fond of garden parties at which they often played croquet or had an archery contest. Croquet's popularity waned as tennis became more popular but it was still enjoyed as an afternoon's entertainment.

Seaside

With the expansion of the railways it became common for families to take an annual trip to the seaside. The wealthy would go for a month or a fortnight and the working classes would go for two or three days. They would go for the sea bathing as it was deemed to be good for their health. There were lodging houses, hotels and houses to rent where they could stay. The wealthy would take their own servants and install them in their rented house.

Whilst they were on holiday they would walk, go on picnics, go boating and sketch. In most seaside towns there were reading rooms, libraries, shops, concert halls and sometimes theatres. There would often be archery contests, the opportunity to go riding, play bowls, croquet and tennis. In the larger resorts there would always be large crowds and they were often frequented by travelling showmen, circuses and Punch and Judy shows. The larger resorts had piers where other entertainments took place.

Bank Holidays and Annual Holidays

In 1871 Parliament passed the Bank Holidays Act which added Easter Monday, Whit Monday, the first Monday in August and Boxing Day as national holidays to Good Friday and Christmas Day. For many Victorians their holidays were unpaid but this gradually changed during the century. By the end of the century some employers gave their employees a short paid holiday after 12 months service. In the North it was customary to close the mills and foundries during Wakes week when the machinery was overhauled. The workers would therefore have a holiday imposed on them. Some poorer families took working holidays and went hop-picking or fruit picking in Kent and other similar places.

Sports and leisure

LESSON PLAN

Unit 11 What was it like for children living in Victorian times?
How did different Victorian children use their spare time?
• to consider how attitudes to children and childhood changed over time

Resources

• Generic sheets 1-2

• Selection of toys – modern and Victorian

• Words for music hall songs

• Puppets for Punch and Judy show

Starting points: whole class

Show the children the two generic sheets and talk to them about the sports they can see represented on them. Discuss the modern version of these sports and the way they are played. Compare the way the Victorians are dressed with how we dress to play these sports nowadays. Talk to the children a little bit about the history of these sports and when they were played.

Teach the children about music halls and the sort of variety acts that would be seen. As a class prepare their own modern music hall acts which they can then present to the rest of the school. They could learn some of the songs that were sung in the music hall and perform them as a whole class within the performance. Alternatively you could get them to write and perform a Punch and Judy show.

In Victorian times children were expected to be seen and not heard. Children nowadays have a far more liberated life and are encouraged to investigate and ask questions. They will already have experienced this difference during their Victorian school day. Encourage them to discuss the merits and downsides to being a child in Victorian times compared to nowadays.

Moving on from how children were expected to behave in the nineteenth century, discuss with the children the annual Victorian holiday and how it compares with modern package holidays. Many of the joys of a seaside holiday for modern children were also enjoyed by Victorian children. However, we have the opportunity to travel abroad and a holiday is not as unusual as it was in those days.

Finally remind the children about the outdoor games that they played during their Victorian day and compare these with their own playground games. They could write a set of rules for the hopscotch, jacks and marbles games they might

have played. If possible, borrow a set of toys from your local museum to look at and compare with their modern toys. The children can sketch them, and then write descriptions of them which can be displayed alongside their drawings.

Group activities

You may wish to copy the activity sheets onto A3 sized paper.

Activity sheet 1
This sheet is for children who need a little more support. They need to write the name of modern and Victorian toys and position them within the correct Venn diagram. They then need to decide whether the Victorian toys would belong to a rich or a poor child. Finally they need to think about what sort of materials the toys are made from.

Activity sheet 2
This sheet is for children who are more confident and work independently. They need to write the name of modern and Victorian toys and position them within the correct Venn diagram. They then need to decide whether the Victorian toys would belong to a rich or a poor child. Finally they will research three other toys.

Activity sheet 3
This sheet is for the most able children. They need to write the name of modern and Victorian toys and position them within the correct Venn diagram. They then need to decide whether the Victorian toys would belong to a rich or a poor child. Next they will research three other toys. Finally they will choose a toy common to the Victorians and modern children and consider how it has developed as time has passed. Once they have done this they will write a paragraph about the toy they have chosen.

Plenary session

Once the children have had plenty of time to complete their worksheets and done some further research bring them back together as a class. Ask the children to compare the results on their Venn diagrams and ask them if there were any toys which they found difficult to classify. They may well all have put the teddy bear in the middle of the diagram so at this point it is worth briefly explaining its origins. Take a vote as a class about whether they would prefer to be a modern child or a Victorian. See if any of the children can explain why they feel this way and draw conclusions about how different aspects of childhood have changed over time.

Ideas for support

The best way to support this unit of work is to have artefacts available for the children to look at and compare with their modern toys. Give them opportunities to play some of the games such as jacks, marbles and hopscotch with other children and talk about what they enjoyed or disliked about these pursuits.

Ideas for extension

To extend the children's understanding of the recreation activities of Victorian children you could ask them to make pictures using shells or pressed flowers. They can design their own cross stitch sampler on squared paper and then stitch it. They would also enjoy making their own thaumatrope or flip book. They could write a set of instructions for others to follow and complete an evaluation of it as a design and technology activity.

Linked ICT activities

There are many websites which the children can access to find out more about Victorian toys. The Virtual Victorians website has a section entitled e-toys which will allow the children to play interactively with a selection of Victorian toys. The Woodlands Junior School website has some useful information about Victorian childhood which summarises many aspects of life for both rich and poor. There is another good website mentioned in the useful resources section which has a simple slideshow which children can access and it shows them photographs of original toys, if you are unable to get hold of any artefacts.

Once the children have looked at these websites they can write a passage using a word processing package. They then need to use spell check and other editing features to refine their writing.

Sports and leisure in Victorian times

Old and modern toys

computer games

toy soldiers

hoop and stick

tea set

reading book

doll

cars

games console

diabolo

musical box

teddy

hopscotch

Noah's Ark

skipping rope

dolls house

scooter

Toys and entertainment

Name ....

1. Look at the pictures on Generic sheet 2. Write the name of each toy in the correct position on the diagram below. Toys that are common to Victorian and modern children need to be in the middle of the diagram.

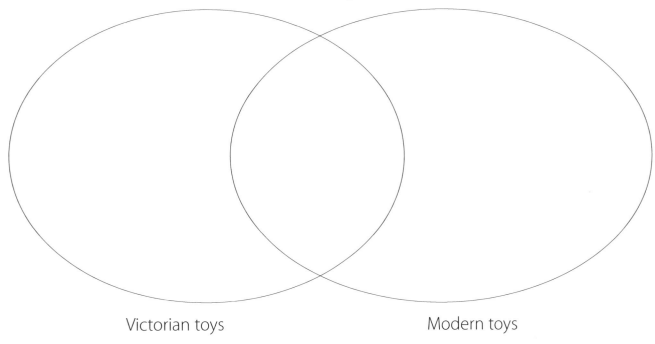

Victorian toys   Modern toys

2. Look at the Victorian toys carefully. Decide which toys would be owned by a rich or a poor child and fill in the chart below.

Toys belonging to a rich child	Toys belonging to a poor child

3. What sort of materials were Victorian toys made from? _____

4. What sort of materials are modern toys made from? _____

_____

Toys and entertainment

Name ....

1. Look at the pictures on Generic sheet 2. Write the name of each toy in the correct position on the diagram below. Toys that are common to Victorian and modern children need to be in the middle of the diagram.

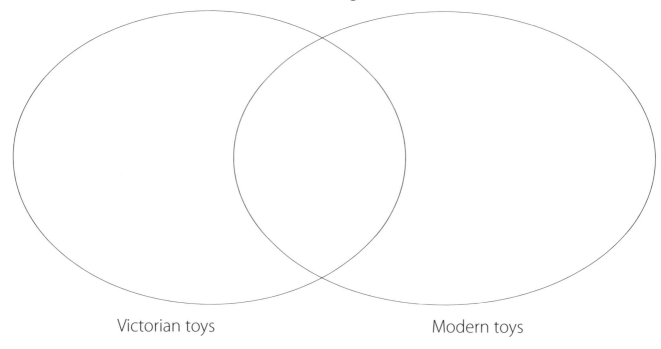

Victorian toys   Modern toys

2. Look at the Victorian toys carefully. Decide which toys would be owned by a rich or a poor child and fill in the chart below.

Toys belonging to a rich child	Toys belonging to a poor child

3. Find out about the following Victorian toys and write a brief description of each: flip book, zoetrope, phenakistoscope, thaumatrope

Toys and entertainment

Name ....

1. Look at the pictures on Generic sheet 2. Write the name of each toy in the correct position on the diagram below. Toys that are common to Victorian and modern children need to be in the middle of the diagram.

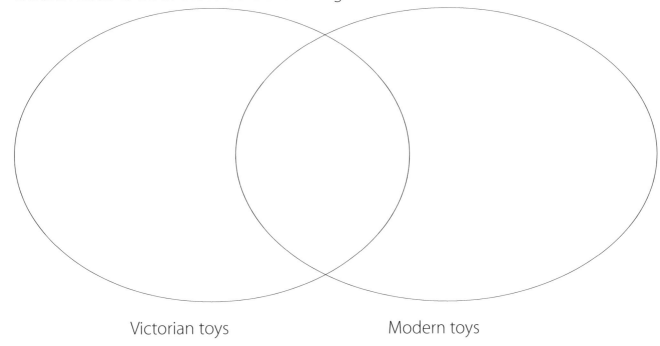

Victorian toys   Modern toys

2. Look at the Victorian toys carefully. Decide which toys would be owned by a rich or a poor child and fill in the chart below.

Toys belonging to a rich child	Toys belonging to a poor child

3. Find out about the following Victorian toys and write a brief description of each:
   flip book, zoetrope, phenakistoscope, thaumatrope

4. Choose a toy that is common to both modern and Victorian children. Compare the two and write a paragraph about how the toy has developed and changed over time.

Health and hygiene

Changes

The nineteenth century was not only a time of change for industry and the way in which people worked and lived, but their health and standards of hygiene began to improve. There was a general awakening during the century that unhygienic conditions caused disease and that improved sanitation could save lives. By the end of the century the Victorians considered prevention more important than a cure. A number of Acts of Parliament were passed during the latter part of the century which helped to improve housing conditions, sanitation, water supplies, ventilation and food supplies. School children were subjected to regular medical inspections and tuberculosis was controlled more successfully than before. Another advance was that patients with infectious diseases were isolated in order to prevent the disease from spreading further.

Despite the many improvements that took place the standard of health care seems a light year behind our modern medical world. Many diseases were undiagnosed as decorum prevented women from undressing in front of men. Infant mortality rates were high and death during childbirth was not uncommon. At the beginning of the century leeches were used as a matter of routine to suck blood from patients and red hot irons were applied to wounds and ulcers in an attempt to help them heal. Such practices seem barbaric and short sighted but we are looking at these from a different world where medical advances are occurring regularly and hospitals have state of the art equipment. In 1911 Parliament passed the National Insurance Act which has developed over the years, and ultimately the National Health Service was created. Before the Act was passed you had to pay for a doctor to visit if you were ill and for the poor this was usually never an option. The wealthy could afford to pay and therefore received treatment but the poor used tried and tested home remedies which often did not work.

Florence Nightingale and women in a man's world

Nursing was not considered to be a reputable occupation until the achievements of Florence Nightingale in the middle of the century. Until that time nurses were poorly paid, overworked and untrained and many were incapable of doing a decent job. Florence Nightingale came from a wealthy family who disapproved of her decision to become a nurse but she was determined. She went to Germany to train and then returned to Britain. In 1854 Britain and France went to the Crimea to support Turkey's military defence against Russia. The soldiers were poorly equipped

and badly organised, and as the campaign continued disease spread. Cholera and dysentery were the biggest killers during the Crimean War and things became so bad that Florence Nightingale was sent out with 38 nurses to try to improve the situation. She arranged and carried out the cleaning of the military hospital that had been set up at Scutari and organised the nursing care properly. As she implemented these changes the death rate began to fall and conditions improved. She became affectionately known as the "Lady with the Lamp" as she used to tour the wards at night talking with and comforting the soldiers in her care. When she returned to Britain she used a fund that had been raised as a result of her deeds to set up a proper nursing school which was based at St. Thomas' Hospital in London. As a result of her selfless efforts nursing became a respectable profession for women.

The fact that women were eventually admitted to universities but not allowed to graduate with a degree has already been mentioned in Chapter 4. Another male bastion was the professional medical world. Women doctors were completely unheard of until an American physician called Elizabeth Blackwell made her mark. There was much disapproval towards her and the first British female doctor, Elizabeth Garrett Anderson. She enrolled as a nursing student at the Middlesex Hospital and attended lectures for men learning to be doctors. She was banned after complaints from them but eventually gained a certificate from the Society of Apothecaries in 1865 which enabled her to practise medicine. They changed the rules after her qualification which prevented other women from following suit. She eventually gained a medical degree from the University of Paris but the British Medical Association failed to acknowledge this. She set up the New Hospital for Women in London which was later renamed after her. In 1876 an Act was passed allowing women to train as doctors but it was not until 1892 that the British Medical Association admitted women as members.

Typhoid, cholera and sanitary improvements

In the Victorian era two of the deadliest diseases were typhoid and cholera. These spread through the poorer areas of towns and cities and were a direct result of poor sanitation. The streets were never cleaned and there were huge dung heaps and piles of rubbish lying around. In the slums people shared a toilet which was often just a bucket or a hole in the ground. These privies frequently overflowed and consequently leaked into wells and polluted the water. The result was "King Cholera" and there was nothing you could do to escape the disease. People used public water pumps to fetch the water they needed for drinking, cooking and washing and so the disease spread. The rivers also became polluted from these insanitary conditions as well as from the by-products of industry.

Edwin Chadwick was a social reformer and he was chairman of the Board of Health which was set up in 1848 to investigate disease and death rates. This was set up as a result of the first Public Health Act which he had been active in pursuing. Another man who influenced changes in sanitary conditions was Sir John Simon. In 1855 he was the first Medical Officer for Health for the City of London. He criticised the water supply and sewage disposal in the city as well as the insanitary behaviour and general lack of cleanliness. By 1865 a complete main drainage system in London had been installed.

Louis Pasteur is best known for his discovery of pasteurisation and vaccination. His discoveries regarding bacteria and pasteurisation lead to discovering a way of purifying sewage. This involved keeping the sewage in an enclosed tank without oxygen in order for anaerobic organisms to get to work. The sewage was then passed through a series of trickling filters and then back to rivers. In 1876 the Rivers Pollution Prevention Act was passed which stated that no untreated sewage could be released into streams or rivers. By 1901 there were street cleaners, clean water, and underground sewers. The sewer system beneath our streets is one of the Victorians' lasting legacies.

Anaesthesia

One of the things we take for granted when we go into hospital, or visit the dentist is anaesthetic. Before the mid 19th century there was no anaesthesia which meant that teeth were extracted without pain relief and if a major operation had to be performed the patient had to be tied to the table to prevent them from moving. During the Victorian era it was discovered that laughing gas (nitrous oxide) could be used for pulling teeth and it made the experience less difficult for the patient. Following on from this discovery a man named William Morton experimented with ether. It was first used during a major operation in 1846 in Massachusetts, then in Britain two months later. It

revolutionised the way in which operations could be performed but there was a problem with the unpleasant after-effects. James Young Simpson used chloroform in 1847 but it took a long time before it was accepted and widely used during procedures. Whilst in labour with her eighth child, Leopold, Queen Victoria used chloroform which lead to it becoming more acceptable.

Antiseptics

Not only were conditions insanitary on the streets and in some homes of Victorian Britain but also within hospitals. There were no sterilised instruments or clothing so even if operations were performed successfully many patients died of gangrene. Louis Pasteur discovered that microorganisms in the air lead to fermentation which leads to infections. His bacteriology investigations lead to the development of an antiseptic system. Joseph Lister, an English surgeon, looked at Pasteur's work and realised that airborne organisms infected open wounds. He started using carbolic acid in his dressings, on instruments and his hands before operating. His critics began to change their minds when they saw that his patients recovered from their operations whilst those of other doctors died. His ideas were slowly accepted and put into practice and many more lives were saved.

Other developments

There were many other medical advances which took place during the nineteenth century such as the invention of aspirin in 1899. Two major discoveries which influenced the development of medicine in the twentieth century were x-rays and the use of radium. Wilhelm Conrad Rœntgen developed the use of x-rays in 1895. Being able to see the bone structure beneath the skin and identify the area that was broken meant that it was possible to mend fractures so that people were no longer permanently crippled from their injuries.

Marie and Pierre Curie discovered radium and polonium at the end of the century. Their pioneering research into radioactive materials was vital for the development of medical treatments for cancer.

Health and hygiene

Unit 11 What was it like for children living in Victorian times?
What was life like for a poor child in the 1840s?
Who helped to improve the lives of Victorian children?
How did life change for children living in Victorian Britain?
- To collect information from a range of sources and draw conclusions about the Victorian period
- to understand that ways of life differed greatly across Victorian society
- to write a narrative using historical detail
- to understand that there are many representations of the Victorian period
- to understand that the work of individuals can change aspects of society
- to find out about important figures in Victorian times
- to recall information about the life of children in Victorian times

Resources

- Generic sheets 1–3

- Non-fiction texts, encyclopaedias, internet access

- Large sheet of paper

Starting points: whole class

To start this topic show the children the first two generic sheets and talk through the impact Florence Nightingale, Edwin Chadwick, Louis Pasteur and Joseph Lister had on the health and hygiene of people in Victorian times. Encourage the children to discuss their achievements and how life was changed in the nineteenth century by them. Spend some time discussing whether the children feel their achievements still have an impact on modern life. Ask them if they can imagine life without sanitary living conditions, and relate it to their rubbish bin collections. What would it be like where they live if their rubbish was not collected or the toilets did not flush?

Next send them away in groups with non-fiction texts, encyclopaedias and allow them access to the internet. Ask them to research the differences in sanitary conditions between rich and poor. The children will hopefully discover that financial status and class did not make any difference when it came to quality of care in hospitals and that infant mortality rates were high whether they were rich or poor. Give them large sheets of paper for them to record the information they have learned and to stick on any pictures or text they wish to include. Once they have finished researching get them to look at what they have written and think about how they could organise this. Finally get the children to write the facts they have discovered as a group report.

Now hold a balloon debate within your classroom. This entails an imaginary hot air balloon with four important characters within it. The idea is that they have to argue their

case as to why they should be allowed to remain in the balloon. Through a series of votes the children will eventually end up with a winner – the figure who has convinced them he/she changed Victorian society the most. Ask for four volunteers to take on the role of one of the four important figures they have been finding out about. You will also need a Chairman who will take overall control of the debate and through whom all the children must pass before being allowed to speak. Allow each of the four figures a chance to speak to the class about how important their role was in Victorian society and how many lives they managed to improve. Once each of them has had a chance to speak the children will take their first vote as to who should be removed from the "balloon" first. After the departure of the first person the floor can be opened and the children allowed the opportunity to question each of the remaining characters. Once they have done this take another vote and remove one more character. When there are only two people left they have one final chance to plead their case and after this the children will cast their final vote to find the winner.

Finally the children's written task will be to distinguish between a fact and an opinion. Help the children to understand the difference by re-reading one of the generic sheets. Ask them whether they think this is a factual account of the major achievements of an individual, or if it is written as someone's personal thoughts about them. Now, ask the children their own opinion of how important their contributions were to the lives of ordinary Victorians.

Group activities

Activity sheet 1
This sheet is for children who need a little more support. They have a list of statements to read and decide which of them are facts and which are opinions. They will need to record their decisions on a piece of paper divided into two sections. After doing this they need to make a list of the differences in the sanitary conditions they live in compared to those of a poor Victorian child.

Activity sheet 2

This sheet is for children who are more confident and work independently. They have a list of statements to read and decide which of them are facts and which are opinions. They will need to record their decisions on a piece of paper divided into two sections and then write a few sentences using the facts about health and hygiene in Victorian times. After doing this they need to make a list of the differences in the sanitary conditions they live in compared to those of a poor Victorian child. Finally they will need to research the lives and achievements of Florence Nightingale or Edwin Chadwick.

Activity sheet 3

This sheet is for the most able children. They have a list of statements to read and decide which of them are facts and which are opinions. They will need to record their decisions on a piece of paper divided into two sections and then write a few sentences using the facts about health and hygiene in Victorian times. After doing this they need to make a list of the differences in the sanitary conditions they live in compared to those of a poor Victorian child. Finally they will need to research the lives and achievements of Florence Nightingale and Edwin Chadwick and write about them.

Plenary session

Look at the finished group reports and decide if they have recorded any of their own opinions or if they have purely recorded facts. What were the major improvements that poor Victorian families would have enjoyed as the century progressed? Compare these changes to the standards that modern children expect.

Ideas for support

If the children are struggling to understand all about the lives and achievements of some of these figures there are visual aids to help them envisage and memorise what they

did in their lives. The BBC website has a lovely section on Florence Nightingale which allows the children to scroll through a summary of her life at their own speed and then answer a quiz to see how much they remember.

In order to help the children to understand how different modern sanitation is from the Victorians write a list of things with them that they use or do to keep healthy. Once they have compiled their list start to research these things and see if they existed in Victorian England, for example, how did they clean their teeth? Did they have toilet paper? Where did their drinking water come from? These similarities and differences should be noted and connected to the children's own everyday experiences. Encourage them to try to envisage what life would have been like without these things which we take for granted.

Ideas for extension

The children could create their own "Top Trump"™ type cards for each medical pioneer of the Victorian era. They could also write about other important figures such as Elizabeth Blackwell, Pierre and Marie Curie, and Wilhelm Conrad Rœntgen for example. These cards should include information such as their dates of birth and death, a précis of their specific contributions and discoveries, a picture and bullet points to summarise their achievements. The children could model these directly on a "Top Trump"™ card if they so wished.

Linked ICT activities

There are websites listed in the Useful Resources section which are valuable for the children to be able to research for their group activity. They are child friendly and suggest links to other useful websites. The children's task will be to use hyperlinks or type in the URL's to find information on this topic. They will then need to use a search engine to find further information.

Florence Nightingale

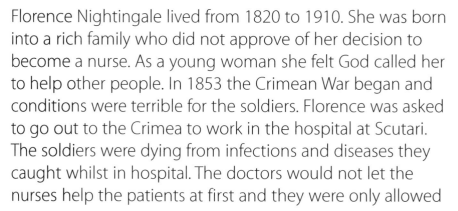

Florence Nightingale lived from 1820 to 1910. She was born into a rich family who did not approve of her decision to become a nurse. As a young woman she felt God called her to help other people. In 1853 the Crimean War began and conditions were terrible for the soldiers. Florence was asked to go out to the Crimea to work in the hospital at Scutari. The soldiers were dying from infections and diseases they caught whilst in hospital. The doctors would not let the nurses help the patients at first and they were only allowed to clean the ward. Eventually they allowed them to help and Florence organised better food, clothing and nursing care. Conditions improved and the soldiers called her the "Lady with the Lamp". When she returned to Britain she was a heroine. She set up a training school for nurses at St. Thomas' Hospital in London and campaigned for better conditions in hospitals.

Edwin Chadwick

Edwin Chadwick lived from 1800 to 1890. He was a social reformer who was very involved in reforming the Poor Laws and ultimately in the improvement of sanitation and public health. He felt that it would cost the country less to improve hygiene and sanitary conditions than to pay for the treatment of those who became ill as a result of their living conditions. Between 1848 and 1849 he was commissioner of the Metropolitan Commission of Sewers in London. When the General Board of Health was set up in 1848 he was one of the commissioners until it was abolished in 1854. Through his efforts and writings pressure was applied to the government so that ultimately sewage systems were built, water supplies were improved and street cleaning took place.

Louis Pasteur

Louis Pasteur lived from 1822 to 1895. He was a famous French chemist and biologist. He discovered the importance of the process of pasteurisation which means that bacteria can be removed from liquid by boiling it then cooling it. He discovered germ theory – that germs and bacteria occur outside the body and then attack the body. He developed a vaccination for rabies and proved that diseases such as tuberculosis and smallpox could be prevented through vaccination.

Joseph Lister

Joseph Lister lived from 1827 to 1912. His discoveries were vital in the development of the antiseptic system and keeping wounds and hospital conditions sterile. He was influenced by Pasteur's findings that bacteria occur in the air. He used a solution of carbolic acid on wounds and surgical instruments to kill bacteria and prevent infection. Many other doctors thought his ideas were not going to work but the success rate of his operations and recovery of his patients were far better than anyone else. In 1879 Listerine mouthwash was named after him.

Victorian slums

How clean and healthy were the Victorians?

Name ....

Look at the following statements and decide which are facts and which are opinions. Record the statements on a piece of paper divided into two sections headed **Fact** and **Opinion**.

1. Florence Nightingale was known as the "Lady with the Lamp".

2. Edwin Chadwick was an important social reformer.

3. Cholera, typhoid and tuberculosis were common diseases during the nineteenth century.

4. Underground sewers are the most important legacy left by the Victorians.

5. The Victorians did not keep clean or live in hygienic conditions.

6. In the city slums several families shared a toilet.

7. Women were allowed to be nurses but it was not a respectable occupation at the beginning of the century.

8. Before Florence Nightingale nurses were untrained and never did their job properly.

9. Florence Nightingale's family disapproved of her becoming a nurse.

10. Poor families lived in unhygienic conditions in towns and in the country.

11. Cholera was spread through a polluted source of water.

12. If you went into hospital for an operation you were likely to develop an infection and die.

13. There was no pain relief during the first half of the nineteenth century and patients were tied to operating tables so they would not move.

14. Landlords did not care what sort of living conditions their tenants had to put up with.

15. The scientific discoveries of Louis Pasteur and Joseph Lister were the most important of the Victorian era.

Think about the progress that has been made since the Victorians in terms of health and hygiene. Write a list of differences between your life and the life of a poor Victorian child.

How clean and healthy were the Victorians?

Name ....

Look at the following statements and decide which of them are facts and which are opinions. Record the statements on a piece of paper divided into two sections headed **Fact** and **Opinion**.

1. Florence Nightingale was known as the "Lady with the Lamp".
2. Edwin Chadwick was an important social reformer.
3. Cholera, typhoid and tuberculosis were common diseases during the nineteenth century.
4. Underground sewers are the most important legacy left by the Victorians.
5. The Victorians did not keep clean or live in hygienic conditions.
6. In the city slums several families shared a toilet.
7. Women were allowed to be nurses but it was not a respectable occupation at the beginning of the century.
8. Before Florence Nightingale nurses were untrained and never did their job properly.
9. Florence Nightingale's family disapproved of her becoming a nurse.
10. Poor families lived in unhygienic conditions in towns and in the country.
11. Cholera was spread through a polluted source of water.
12. If you went into hospital for an operation you were likely to develop an infection and die.
13. There was no pain relief during the first half of the nineteenth century and patients were tied to operating tables so they would not move.
14. Landlords did not care what sort of living conditions their tenants had to put up with.
15. The scientific discoveries of Louis Pasteur and Joseph Lister were the most important of the Victorian era.

Once you have separated the facts from the opinions write a few sentences about health and hygiene in Victorian times.

Think about the progress that has been made since the Victorians in terms of health and hygiene. Write a list of differences between your life and the life of a poor Victorian child.

Find out more about Florence Nightingale or Edwin Chadwick and write a list of facts about them and their achievements.

How clean and healthy were the Victorians?

Name ....

Look at the following statements and decide which of them are facts and which are opinions. Record the statements on a piece of paper divided into two sections headed **Fact** and **Opinion**.

1. Florence Nightingale was known as the "Lady with the Lamp".
2. Edwin Chadwick was an important social reformer.
3. Cholera, typhoid and tuberculosis were common diseases during the nineteenth century.
4. Underground sewers are the most important legacy left by the Victorians.
5. The Victorians did not keep clean or live in hygienic conditions.
6. In the city slums several families shared a toilet.
7. Women were allowed to be nurses but it was not a respectable occupation at the beginning of the century.
8. Before Florence Nightingale nurses were untrained and never did their job properly.
9. Florence Nightingale's family disapproved of her becoming a nurse.
10. Poor families lived in unhygienic conditions in towns and in the country.
11. Cholera was spread through a polluted source of water.
12. If you went into hospital for an operation you were likely to develop an infection and die.
13. There was no pain relief during the first half of the nineteenth century and patients were tied to operating tables so they would not move.
14. Landlords did not care what sort of living conditions their tenants had to put up with.
15. The scientific discoveries of Louis Pasteur and Joseph Lister were the most important of the Victorian era.

Once you have separated the facts from the opinions write a paragraph about health and hygiene in Victorian times.

Think about the progress that has been made since the Victorians in terms of health and hygiene. Write a list of differences between your life and the life of a poor Victorian child.

Find out more about Florence Nightingale or Edwin Chadwick and write about their lives, their achievements and their legacy.

CHAPTER 10

Looking for evidence of the Victorians

Evidence on the streets

Throughout this book the children will have learned about the everyday lives of the Victorians and should have an insight into how things have changed over time. This chapter focuses on the children identifying and discovering the evidence left behind by the Victorians. The legacy left by the Victorians did not end with their medical, hygiene and industrial discoveries and inventions. Most towns still have some evidence of the past if the children look closely enough.

Even if there is little evidence of Victorian architecture where the children live a street name often gives away a hint of a settlement's past. Even the small town where I live has a Victoria Road and an Albert Street. Other names to look out for are those of Victorian Prime Ministers, such as Disraeli, Gladstone, as well as those commemorating the Boer War – Ladysmith, Kimberley, Mafeking, and the Crimean War – Alma, Inkerman, Sebastopol. If you are extremely lucky you may be able to find a post box from this era. The initials on the front of the letter box indicate which King or Queen was on the throne at the time of their installation.

Much evidence of the Victorians can still be observed above people's heads. We rarely stop and look up at buildings in our locality and really look at what is above us. Many buildings in High Streets for example have the date of their construction embedded in stone. Where there are new developments much of this evidence is destroyed but some houses in residential areas may have a date themselves.

Another important feature of Victorian buildings is the earthenware chimney pots. Some of these chimney pots are very ornate and clearly made by skilled craftsmen who took pride in finishing off their work even if no-one saw it on a daily basis.

In larger towns and cities you are likely to find large public buildings built by the Victorians such as churches, stations and town halls. Near these buildings you may be able to see statues of famous local people, or plaques recording information about people or events in the past. Another valuable place to visit is a graveyard. The memorials in a church and the gravestones can reveal a lot of information about the people who lived in the locality. Stonemasons were skilled craftsmen and their work will be in evidence in these places.

When looking at domestic Victorian buildings there are a number of features that identify their age. The Victorians started to use coloured bricks and they used these to create decorative brickwork. If you look at a row of more affluent terraced Victorian housing this will become apparent. They also often decorated the bargeboards just below the roof line.

Poorer Victorian housing was set within much narrower streets whereas for the more affluent they had large detached houses in wide streets lined with trees. Some of the poorer dwellings can still be found close to industrial areas or railway lines. Little "two up two down" dwellings without gardens still exist but you need to look round corners and down narrow streets to find them.

Many houses had a bay window at the front because the window tax was abolished in 1851, and some had a basement below street level which could be reached via a set of steps. The street furniture is also a good indication of when the area was constructed. The Victorians were fond of using iron work so there were a lot of iron railings, lamp posts, boot scrapers, coal-hole covers and the door furniture also reflected this trend.

Within towns you can sometimes find evidence of Victorian commerce if signs and hoardings are preserved. Even if the original signage has disappeared you may still find signs such as that of a pawnbroker, which is three golden spheres hanging from a bar. Many towns have public houses with names which give away their age and origins which has already been mentioned in an earlier chapter.

Styles of architecture

The Victorians favoured two main styles of architecture to build their towns and cities, Classical and Gothic. These styles are most evident on the grander public buildings they constructed. Classical architecture was influenced by Greek and Roman temples and the buildings were adorned with columns and domes. The Gothic style on the other hand was influenced by medieval or fairytale castles with their pointed turrets and narrow arched windows.

Comparing then and now

If you visit a town which grew during the Victorian era there will be a huge number of changes to the architecture and use of the buildings over time. In order to understand fully how dramatic these changes are find two pictures of the same place, one from the twenty first century and one from the nineteenth. Observe the differences in the chimneys, the street surface, the clothing of the passers-by, the traffic, the street sellers and the shop fronts, and then look to see what has remained the same for over one hundred years. Like the Romans the Victorians shaped the world as we know it today even if we do not notice little clues on a daily basis. The buildings may no longer be there but the demarcation of the roads and layout of the town may still be there as it was when the town planners first started.

Looking for evidence of the Victorians

Unit 12 How did life change in our locality in Victorian times?
What evidence of Victorian times remains in our area?
- to identify and record characteristic features of Victorian buildings
- to recognise ways in which buildings have been changed over time, and consider reasons for the changes

Resources

- Generic sheets 1-2

- Interactive whiteboard and link to the internet

- Clipboards, pencils etc

- Photos of a town in Victorian times and as it is today

- Pictures of buildings from various points in time

- Selection of building materials

- Non-fiction texts about architecture, Victorian homes and William Morris

Starting points: whole class

The first thing you need to do with the children is show them the following website http://www.woodlands-junior. kent.sch.uk/Homework/houses/victorian.htm and work through the photographs and questions. It has clear photographic examples of Victorian houses and walks the children through each aspect a little at a time. The questions are useful additions to the facts that are presented on each page and the children will be able to recognise features they are familiar with already.

Once you have spent some time working through the pictures and have identified the main features of Victorian housing ask the children about their own experience. Some of them may live in a Victorian house themselves or visit one. If you are fortunate your school may be within an area of Victorian housing and the children see these features every day. Whatever their experience ask them to tell you what they have noticed and where they have seen it. Now show them generic sheet 2 from Chapter 7 and ask them if they can identify as many different features of a Victorian house as possible. You could give them a time limit and a copy of the sheet each and ask them to label each different feature.

The most important thing to do now is to get the children out and looking for Victorian features somewhere in their locality. Show them generic sheet 1 with all the different shapes and styles of chimney pot. This will give them an

idea of the sort of chimney that will identify a house as Victorian. The simpler plainer chimney pots they may see are more likely to be on newer houses. Make up a question sheet which gives them clear instructions about what to look for during their field trip. It should include questions such as:

1. Find a building with a date during the Victorian era. What is the building used for now?

2. What do you think it was used for during the nineteenth century?

3.a Find a typical Victorian terraced house or villa. Sketch the front of the house.

3.b List the typical Victorian features you can see. Are there any modern additions to the house?

This activity sheet will need to be tailored to the area you live in and the specific buildings that are there. When they return from their visit ensure they have time to complete and refine the sketches they made and write up their findings. Provide them all with a copy of generic sheet 2 which is a simple "I-Spy" type record of what they see as well.

After investigating their local area the children can build on what they have observed by completing the group activity sheets.

Group activities

Activity sheet 1
This sheet is for children who need a little more support. It asks them to consider the differences and similarities between modern and Victorian building materials. They need to think about why Victorian houses rarely have their original windows and then they are asked to do some research into the two main styles of architecture favoured by the Victorians.

Activity sheet 2
This sheet is for children who are more confident and work independently. It asks them to consider the differences and similarities between modern and Victorian building materials. They are asked to think about how modern

owners adapt Victorian houses and why. Finally they are asked to do some research into the two main styles of architecture favoured by the Victorians.

Activity sheet 3
This sheet is for the most able children. It asks them to consider the differences and similarities between modern and Victorian building materials. They are encouraged to think about the properties of some modern building materials and why they are used. They are asked to think about how modern owners adapt Victorian houses and why. Next they are asked about whether public buildings are used for the same purpose as the Victorians, and why. Finally they are asked to do some research into the two main styles of architecture favoured by the Victorians.

Plenary session

Show the children some pictures of different buildings, modern, Victorian as well as others from other eras and ask them to try to identify at which point in history they were constructed. Encourage them to give you clear reasons for their answers using evidence from the pictures. These pictures should be added to your suspended timeline in the appropriate place.

Ideas for support

To support the children's learning about Victorian building materials get hold of a selection of different materials, terracotta tiles, slate, brick, uPVC, and if possible a double glazed window unit. Get the children to handle the materials and think about how they are made and the raw

materials that are used. Look around the school building and try to identify the different materials that are used and the purpose they serve. If you are lucky enough to be in a Victorian school building look at how it has been adapted and think about the reasons why.

Ideas for extension

In order to extend some of the children even further you can ask them to consider the inside of an affluent Victorian home and compare it with their modern homes. The rooms were given different names, the parlour, nursery, and so on and had specific purposes and times when they were used. Ask the children to find out about the layout of such a house and the articles of furniture that they would expect to see.

You could also introduce the children to the work of William Morris and how he influenced the internal decoration of a house. They could copy some of his patterns and design some of their own wallpaper and fabric in the same style.

Linked ICT activities

The ICT activity that has already been covered during the main class activity is of value. The children could create their own fact file on Victorian buildings and architecture using copy and paste techniques in a Word document. They should search for photographs or pictures of examples they are writing about and paste them into their writing.

The children should also use geometric tools in a graphics package to draw a specific feature of a Victorian building. This drawing should then be imported into their Word document.

Victorian chimney pots

Victorian I-Spy

❏ Boot scraper

❏ Decorative brickwork

❏ Bargeboards

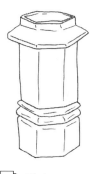

❏ Chimney pot

❏ Finial

❏ Iron railings

❏ Bay window

❏ Terraced houses

❏ Post box

❏ Stained glass

Victorian architecture

Name

1. List five characteristics of Victorian buildings:

2. What sort of building materials were used by the Victorians and in modern buildings? List them below:

3. What sort of modern building materials do we use now that are different from the Victorians?

4. Why do you think people living in Victorian houses usually change their windows?

5. Do some research and then write a short paragraph about each of the following styles of architecture.

CLASSICAL

GOTHIC

Victorian architecture

Name ....

1. List the main characteristics of Victorian buildings:

2. What sort of building materials were used by the Victorians and in modern buildings? List them below.

3. What sort of modern building materials do we use now that are different from the Victorians? Why are these materials used instead?

4. What sort of alterations do people make to Victorian houses nowadays? Why do you think they make these changes?

5. Do some research into each of the following styles of architecture.

CLASSICAL

GOTHIC

Write a short passage about each with a sketch or picture of a building in each of these styles.

Victorian architecture

Name ....

1. What sort of building materials were used by the Victorians and in modern buildings? List them below:

2. What sort of modern building materials do we use now that are different from the Victorians? Why are these materials used instead? What properties do they have which make them more useful?

3. What sort of alterations do people make to Victorian houses nowadays? Why do you think they make these changes?

4. Are public buildings used for the same purpose as they were in the Victorian era? Why do you think this is?

5. Do some research into each of the following styles of architecture.

   CLASSICAL

   GOTHIC

Write a short passage about each with a sketch or picture of a building in each of these styles.

Name some well known public buildings which are built in each of these styles.

Answers

CHAPTER 5 (Generic sheet 1)

1. 1825 Steam train

2. 1843 Propellor driven steamship

3. 1863 Internal combustion engine

4. 1870 Penny Farthing bicycle

5. 1885 Petrol driven car

6. 1888 Pneumatic tyres

7. 1890 Electric tram

CHAPTER 6

2. Eight people lived at 3, Railway Cottages. Five of them were children.

3. A bobbin carrier supplied the looms with bobbins for spinning and weaving.
    A carder prepared the wool for weaving.
    A piecer joined together broken threads on spinning machines.
    A scavenger picked up loose cotton from underneath the machinery and cleaned the mechanism of excess oil, dirt and dust.
    A spinner had to run up and down a row of machines repairing broken threads and snags.
    A weaver was responsible for setting up the looms for the cloth to be woven.

4. Four of the residents were weavers, Robert Jarvis, Charlotte Jarvis, Eliza Wingfield and Charles Miller.

5. Five children aged 12 and under worked in the cotton mill.

6. The older children were piecers and the younger ones were scavengers.

7. The Wingfield family had three generations living under the same roof.

8. Charles Miller's father had died so he was the head of the family. We know his father had died because Harriet Miller was a widow.

9. It is likely that James Miller was ill or disabled from an injury and so could not work.

10. Eleanor Dearden was widowed and lived with her daughter, son-in-law and grandchildren. She was not a factory worker and so would be at home with the younger children.

CHAPTER 8

Victorian toys
hoop and stick
diabolo

Both
doll
books
skipping rope
hopscotch
Noah's Ark
toy soldiers
musical box
dolls house
tea set

Modern toys
teddy bear
scooter
games console
cars

CHAPTER 9

Fact
Florence Nightingale was known as the "Lady with the Lamp".

Edwin Chadwick was an important social reformer.

Cholera, typhoid and tuberculosis were common diseases during the nineteenth century.

In the city slums several families shared a toilet.

Women were allowed to be nurses but it was not a respectable occupation at the beginning of the century.

Florence Nightingale's family disapproved of her becoming a nurse.

Cholera was spread through a polluted source of water.

There was no pain relief during the first half of the nineteenth century and patients were tied to operating tables so they would not move.

Opinion

Underground sewers are the most important legacy left by the Victorians.

The Victorians did not keep clean or live in hygienic conditions.

Before Florence Nightingale nurses were untrained and never did their job properly.

Poor families lived in unhygienic conditions in towns and in the country.

If you went into hospital for an operation you were likely to develop an infection and die.

Landlords did not care what sort of living conditions their tenants had to put up with.

The scientific discoveries of Louis Pasteur and Joseph Lister were the most important of the Victorian era.

CHAPTER 10

Victorian building materials
brick, wood, slate, glass, iron, steel

Modern building materials
uPVC, plasterboard, concrete, aluminium, fibreglass, insulation, breeze blocks, double glazing

Glossary

Chapter 1

empire	a large number of states or countries under a single authority
era	a specific period of time
monarch	the King or Queen
typhoid fever	an infectious bacterial disease

Chapter 2

blacking factory	a factory producing shoe polish
cholera	an infectious bacterial disease which causes severe sickness and diarrhoea
epidemic	a disease which spreads amongst a community
legislation	the process of law making
overseer	the supervisor of a group of workers
protestants	Christians who do not follow the Roman Catholic faith
reforms	improvements and changes

Chapter 3

bodice	the part of a dress above the waist
buttonhook	a metal hook used to do up the buttons on boots
corset	a tight undergarment to support the abdomen
crinoline	a stiffened, hooped petticoat
pantaloons	tight fitting trousers which fasten below the foot or the calf
perambulator	a pram
smock	a loose shirt which is gathered at the top with tiny pleats

Chapter 4

boarding school	a school where pupils live during term time
corporal punishment	a punishment such as beating
governess	a woman who lived in a private home and taught the children
preparatory school	a private school preparing children for a higher school
tutor	a private teacher

Chapter 5

brougham	a carriage pulled by horses with a driver perched outside
clipper	a fast sailing ship
hackney cab	a vehicle for hire, a taxi
hansom cab	a 2 wheeled carriage for 2 people inside and a driver behind
Industrial Revolution	the development of industry in the late 18th century and early 19th century
landau	a 4 wheeled carriage with a removable cover
navvies	labourers who built railways, roads and canals
phaeton	a light open carriage pulled by 2 horses
pneumatic	filled with compressed air
rolling stock	the carriages and engines on a railway

Chapter 6

bobbin	a cylindrical reel which holds thread
carder	a person who combed fibres prior to weaving or spinning
census	the official count of the population every 10 years
coke	the residue left behind after coal extraction
flax	a plant whose fibres are used in the textile industry
fly maker	a person who made the shuttles for the looms
foundries	a factory where metal is cast
hydraulic	a mechanism operated by a liquid
migration	movement from one place to another
piecer	a person who joined together broken threads on spinning machines
scavenger	a child who picked up loose cotton from underneath the machinery and cleaned the mechanism of excess oil, dirt and dust
Spinning Jenny	a machine which spun with more than one spindle
Spinning Mule	a hybrid form of the Spinning Jenny and the Water Frame that could be powered by a steam engine
Trade Union	an organisation to protect workers in a trade or profession

Chapter 7

apprentice	a person who is learning a trade on the job
match girls	young girls who sold matches on the street to earn a living
mudlarking	searching river mud for valuable objects to sell
slums	overcrowded and insanitary areas of housing
tannery	a place where animal hides are converted into leather
workhouse	a place where the destitute lived and worked for their board and lodging

Chapter 8

Harlequinade	the part of a pantomime where a Harlequin appeared
pantomime	a theatrical production at Christmas based on a fairy tale or traditional story
sphairistike	an early form of tennis
Wakes week	an annual holiday in the industrial north of England

Chapter 9

anaerobic organism	an organism that lives without oxygen
anaesthesia	a means of causing insensitivity to pain by using gas or drugs
bacteriology	the study of bacteria
chloroform	a liquid used as an anaesthetic
Crimean war	a conflict which took place from 1853 to 1856 against the Russian Empire
fermentation	the breakdown of a substance by micro-organisms
gangrene	the decomposition of body tissue
pasteurisation	the process of heating a liquid to sterilise it
polonium	a radioactive metallic element
radium	a radioactive metallic element
sanitary	conditions which are clean and healthy
tuberculosis	a bacterial disease which affects the lungs
vaccination	inoculation to cause immunity from a disease
ventilation	the circulation of air

Chapter 10

bargeboard	a board hiding the ends of roof timbers
finial	the ornament at the apex of a roof
nursery	a room for young children
parlour	a sitting room in a house
pawnbroker	a person who lends money in exchange for personal property
stonemason	a person who cuts and builds with stone

Useful resources

Places to visit

Acton Scott Historic Working Farm	Shropshire
Balmoral Castle	nr. Ballater, Grampians
Castell Coch	nr. Cardiff, South Glamorgan
Clifton Suspension Bridge	Bristol, Avon
Hughenden Manor	Buckinghamshire
Lanhydrock	Bodmin, Cornwall
Linley Sambourne House	Kensington, London
Osborne House	East Cowes, Isle of Wight
Penrhyn Castle	Bangor, Gwynedd
Quarry Bank Mill	Wilmslow, Cheshire
Royal Albert Bridge	Saltash, Cornwall
SS Great Britain	Bristol, Avon
Standen	East Grinstead, West Sussex
Tenement House	Glasgow
Waddesdon Manor	Aylesbury, Buckinghamshire
Wightwick Manor	Wolverhampton, West Midlands

Museums and Exhibitions

Beamish Open Air Museum	County Durham
The Charles Dickens Museum	London
Florence Nightingale Museum	Lambeth Palace Road, London
Fox Talbot Museum	Lacock Abbey, nr. Chippenham, Wilts
Grove Museum	nr. Ramsey, Isle of Man
Gunnersbury Park Museum	Acton, London
Ironbridge Gorge Museum	Telford, Shropshire
Kew Bridge Steam Museum	Brentford, Middlesex
Levant Mine and Beam Museum	Levant, nr. St. Just, Cornwall
Milestones	Basingstoke, Hampshire
National Trust Museum of Childhood	Sudbury, Derbyshire
Preston Hall Museum	Stockton-on-Tees, Cleveland
Rossendale Museum	Rossendale, Lancashire
Museum of Childhood	Edinburgh
Museum of the Great Western Railway	Swindon, Wiltshire
Museum of London	London Wall, London
Victoria and Albert Museum	South Kensington, London
York Castle Museum	York

Bibliography

How did your locality change in Victorian times? – Jill Barber
(London: Evans Brothers Ltd)

Investigating the Victorians – Alison Honey
(London: The National Trust Enterprises Ltd)

The Victorians - Britain Through the Paintings of the Age –
Jeremy Paxman (London: BBC Books)

A History of Everyday Things in England 1851-1914 –
Marjorie and C.H.B. Quennell (London: B.T. Batsford Ltd)

History Makers of the Industrial Revolution – Nigel Smith
(Hove: Wayland Publishers Ltd)

Streets in Victorian Times – Margaret Stephen
(Hove: Wayland Publishers Ltd)

Daily Life in a Victorian house – Laura Wilson
(London: Hamlyn Children's Books)

The Victorians – Tim Wood
(Loughborough: Ladybird Books Ltd)

Queen Victoria – J.R.C. Yglesias
(Loughborough: Ladybird Books Ltd)

Websites

Chapter 1
http://www.victorianweb.org/painting/gallery/victoria.html
www.npg.org.uk
The National Portrait Gallery has some excellent photos of
portraits of Queen Victoria.

www.legacyfamilytree.com
Software for making family trees.

Chapter 2
www.barnardos.org.uk
The website for the charity Barnardo's.

www.unicef.org.uk
The website for the charity Unicef.

www.bbc.co.uk/schools/primaryhistory/victorian_britain
An excellent website with games, information and quizzes
about the working lives of children in Victorian Britain.

Chapter 3
www.bbc.co.uk/history/british/launch_gms_victorian_dress.shtml
A webpage where you can play a game to dress a Tudor and
a Victorian correctly.

Chapter 4
www.beamish.org.uk/Home.aspx
The website for the Beamish Open Air Museum.

www.beamishcollections.com/literacy.html
A website with an Education Literacy pack to support work
on Victorian schools.

Chapter 5
www.ordnancesurvey.co.uk
You can access small portions of maps all over the United
Kingdom using a postcode and location on this website.

*http://leisure.ordnancesurvey.co.uk/products/historical-maps/
historical-maps-historical-1-inch-to-1-mile*
You can purchase historical maps of your area through
this website.

Chapter 6
*http://primary.espressohome.co.uk/espresso/modules/www/
history/james_watt/index.html*
This has an animated story about James Watt and how his
steam engine works.

www.beamishcollections.com/education/Learning/Mining.asp
This web page has some interesting photos of mining in
Victorian times.

www.beamishcollections.com/george%20stephenson.html
There are interactive whiteboard resources, worksheets etc
about George Stephenson through this link.

Chapter 7
*www.bbc.co.uk/schools/primaryhistory/victorian_britain/rich_and_
poor_families*
There are resources here about the role of a governess, and
also about children working as apprentices in a textile mill.

www.victorians.org.uk
The Virtual Victorians website allows the children to look at
what a factory worker's family did each day of the week.

Chapter 8
www.victorians.org.uk
There is a section entitled e-toys which allows the children
to play interactively with a selection of Victorian toys.

www.woodlands-junior.kent.sch.uk/Homework/victorians/
children/index.htm
The Woodlands Junior School website has some useful
information about Victorian childhood.

www.topmarks.co.uk/slideshows/victorians.htm
This simple slideshow of original toys is ideal for children
who are unable to see any artefacts.

Chapter 9
www.bbc.co.uk/schools/famouspeople/standard/nightingale
This allows the children to scroll through a potted history
of the life of Florence Nightingale with a quiz at the end to
see how much they remember.

www.woodlands-junior.kent.sch.uk/Homework/victorians/florence/
index.htm
This also gives another brief history of Florence
Nightingale.

www.sciencemuseum.org.uk/broughttolife/people/
edwinchadwick.aspx
This is a page of information about Edwin Chadwick and
his achievements.

www.bbc.co.uk/history/historic_figures/pasteur_louis.shtml
This is a page of information about Louis Pasteur.

http://web.ukonline.co.uk/b.gardner/Lister.html
This is a page of information about Joseph Lister.

Chapter 10
www.woodlands-junior.kent.sch.uk/Homework/houses/
victorian.htm
This website has excellent photographic examples of the
features of Victorian houses. As you progress through each
section the children are given questions to answer.

Other useful sites

www.npg.org.uk/webquests
There are 2 exellent sections on "The Great Exhibition"
and "Victorian Magic Latern". These webquests present the
children with challenges to fulfill whilst giving them
information in a variety of formats to interact with and use
to create a piece of work.

ICT Resources

CD-Rom
Microsoft Encarta

Software
Microsoft Word – word processing package

Textease CT Studio
Lightbox Education, Friar Gate Studios, Ford Street, Derby,
DE1 1EE. Tel: 01332 258381. Fax: 01332 258382

TV programmes and DVDs

The Victorians – Jeremy Paxman	BBC DVD
Victorian Farm	BBC DVD
Victorian Flower Garden	BBC DVD
Victorian Kitchen	BBC DVD
Victorian Kitchen Garden	BBC DVD

Notes

Notes

Notes